2-46

What a Modern Catholic
Believes About
GOD

by

Andrew M. Greeley

The Thomas More Press
Chicago, Illinois

For Andy and Mary Burd

Contents

Introduction

I SHALL SPEAK OF.GOD. I shall not argue about his existence, for such an argument is one of the most foolish enterprises on which man has embarked. Everyone, as I will point out in the next chapter, has his own God. The argument about whether there is a God is but an extremely useful escape from the question of who he is. It is on the subject of who he is that I propose to speak.

I shall describe the God of the Christians, but as does anyone who speaks of God, I will necessarily speak of *my* God. Whoever proposes to speak of God necessarily writes out of his own personal experience of God. Even the most dry and abstract of philosophers is still writing about his God and his experience of God, however much he may have hidden the experience beneath abstruse theoretical prose. To write of God is to write of one's self and one's experience of the transcendent. Since we cannot do otherwise, it is appropriate for us to acknowledge this fact at the very beginning of whatever we say about God.

I will confess that I have rediscovered God, or perhaps even discovered him for the first time, though I do not believe that such an experience is unique to me. Everyone who gives any thought to the ultimate issues of life is in a constant process of rediscovering God or of discovering him for the first time. But there is something a little unusual about my rediscovery of God, for I have rediscovered him not through the writings of the philosophers and the theologians, most of whom presently seem to have had very little experience with him, but rather through the writings of the social scientists; in particular, through the writings of men like Clifford Geertz and Mircea Eliade. Indeed, I think the anthropologists and the historians of religion may very well know far more about God than do most of the philosophers and the theologians.

Blaise Pascal once rejected the God of the philosophers and the geometricians in favor of the God of Abraham and the God of Isaac and the God of Jacob. I often wonder what Pascal would think of the God of the social scientists. The tools of social scientific analysis provide us with the resources for understanding who the God of Abraham and Isaac and Jacob is in our own time; that is no small contribution - particularly since the philosophers and the theologians seem quite incapable of providing such tools. So perhaps Pascal would look more kindly on the social scientists than he did on the philosophers and the geometricians. Whether he would or not, this book, nonetheless, is a study of God from the point of view of the social scientist.

I shall be anthropomorphic in my description of God even though philosophers like Leslie Dewart and Michael Novak will be horrified by such language, as will theologians like Bishop Robinson. However if man is to speak of God at all - and he must - he has no choice but to speak of him in human terms. The Novaks and the Robinsons of the world insist that such human terms and images are inadequate to cope with the notion of God, and of course they are right, though this is not a new discovery on their part. But as such scholars as Sten Stensen and Langdon Gilkey have noted in response to those who are hung up on the language problem, mytho-poetic language is as valid in its own context as any other form of human language. If man has always used mytho-poetic and anthropomorphic language to speak of God, it has always been with the realization of the inadequacy of the language - we did not need Mr. Novak to learn this – and also with the realization that however inadequate his language might be he still had to speak of God.

I shall not be "serious" in my discussion of God, and this will offend both theists and atheists who believe that the subject of the deity must necessarily be serious. But just as the sober language of rational and empirical science is inadequate to cope with God, so is the stolid, dull language of "scientific" philosophy and theology. Professor Sten Stensen tells us the language which man uses to describe God is the same as the language he uses to tell jokes, and that is, I think, as it should be. When the Christian is asked whether his God is "serious" or not he must respond that he is not serious, that Gilbert Keith Chesterton was right in suggesting that God was a joker and that the subject of man's relationship with God is something of such importance that it cannot be treated with anything but laughter.

I shall rely heavily in this volume on poetic imagery; mostly the poetic imagery of the Scriptures as, alas, I am capable of very little poetic imagery of my own. I argue that poetry is necessary to describe God because the ordinary language of everyday conversation simply is inadequate to even begin to deal with the reality that is God.

Ours is a sober, serious, rational, scientific world. When a man says he proposes to speak with wit, poetry, mythology, and anthropomorphic images, the world says that the man is not "serious," or that what he is trying to describe is "not for real." But as I hope to argue later on in this book, when man wishes to speak about the "Really Real" he has no choice but to abandon serious, sober, rational, scientific language. The Really Real – that is, the Ultimate Reality – can only be described in a way that begins to be satisfactory when one uses the language of poetry, the dance, music, and ecstasy. That the so-called modern world has no understanding of such language is not a reflection on those who use such language but on the modern world itself.

This is a book about the "images" of God. It is an attempt to explain the implications of the images. For those readers who don't believe in images, there will be little consolation in this volume. I can only suggest that they go back to their mathematical theorems. The world in which most real men live is filled with imagery, both conscious and unconscious. Science claims to withdraw from image in order to be about its precise, rationalistic tasks. The tasks of science are admirable, yet, as historians and philosophers of science such as Michael Polanyi and Thomas Kuhn have observed, the great scientific discoveries and revolutions have been made not by men who have withdrawn from the language and the insight of emotion, but rather by men who were able to bring emotion and imagery – indeed, passionate and emotional imagery – to the scientific quest. But however necessary unemotional, dispassionate, sober language is for the endeavors of positive science, it will simply not do when man is wrestling with the questions of the meaning and purpose of life, which is simply another way of describing the God question.

Enough of preliminary arguments with those misguided souls who would forbid us to speak of God or, indeed, of anything which cannot be reduced to a scientific theorem. Let us get on with our work of examining images. And let us begin with three images from poets writing in the Jewish-Christian tradition: an image of the Father, and one of the Son, and one of the Holy Spirit.

In his remarkable play *Gideon,* Paddy Chayefsky records the following dialogue between Gideon and God:

GIDEON

I thought of nothing but you the whole night. I am possessed by all the lunacy of love. If I could, I would cover you with veils, God, and keep you hidden behind the curtains in my tent. Oh! Just say again you love me, God.

THE ANGEL

I do, Gideon.

GIDEON

I do not know why. I must say, I do not know why.

THE ANGEL

I hardly know why myself, but then passion is an unreasonable thing.[1]

Even to those of us who are familiar with the language of the Jewish and Christian traditions, Chayefsky's rephrasing of the image of God the Father is startling. As we shall see in a later chapter, it would be horrifying, even blasphemous, in other religious traditions, for Chayefsky's God is "hung up" on man. He is emotionally involved with this bizarre creature of his to such an extent that Chayefsky even has him suggest that he doesn't quite know why he has become so "hung up" on man. We in the Jewish and Christian religious traditions are plagued with a God who will not - indeed even *cannot* - leave us alone. Such an image is perhaps the most revolutionary one in the

---

[1]Paddy Chayefsky, *Gideon*. New York: ©Random House, 1961, p. 67.

whole history of human religion.

Another version of the same image, and one this time we will appropriate to God the Son, is to be found in Francis Thompson's classic *Hound of Heaven,* a poem which is worth quoting here once again if only because when we first read it we probably believed that the image was an exaggeration of the reality; but, in fact, the faith of the Christian is that the image is far less than the reality.

....

I fled Him, down the nights and down the days;
    I fled Him, down the arches of the years;
I fled Him, down the labyrinthine ways
    Of my own mind; and in the mist of tears
I hid from Him, and under running laughter.
        Up vistaed hopes I sped;
        And shot, precipitated,
Adown Titanic glooms of chasmed fears,
    From those strong Feet that followed, followed after.

        But with unhurrying chase,
        And unperturbed pace
Deliberate speed, majestic instancy,
        They beat - and a Voice beat
        More instant than the Feet -
'All things betray thee, who betrayest Me.

....

        Now of that long pursuit
        Comes on at hand the bruit;
That Voice is round me like a bursting sea:
        'And is thy earth so marred,
        Shattered in shard on shard?
Lo, all things fly thee, for thou fliest Me!
Strange, piteous, futile thing!

Wherefore should any set thee love apart?
Seeing none but I makes much of naught' (He said)
'And human love needs human meriting:
    How has thou merited –
Of all man's clotted clay the dingiest clot?
    Alack, thou knowest not
How little worthy of any love thou art!
Whom wilt thou find to love ignoble thee,
    Save me, save only Me?
All which I took from thee I did but take,
    Not for thy harms,
But just that thou might'st seek it in My arms.
    All which thy child's mistake
Fancies as lost, I have stored for thee at home;
    Rise, clasp My hand, and come!

    Halts by me that footfall:
    Is my gloom, after all,
Shade of His hand, outstretched caressingly?
    'Ah, fondest, blindest, weakest,
    I am He whom thou seekest!
Thou dravest love from thee, who dravest Me.

With unperturbed pace the Hound of Heaven pursues
us. Down the nights and down the years through the
dark troubled halls of our souls he keeps coming. He
is not an aloof God in Heaven, disinterested in our behavior; not a cantankerous God waiting for us to vio-
late some of his rules, sure that he may become angry
at us. He is not a great hangman in the sky, nor an
old Irish monsignor breaking up dances at the cross-
roads. He is an insistent lover, pursuing us with per-
sistent deliberate speed despite our own frenzied and
foolish attempts to escape from him. He is a real
problem, this pushy Jewish God of ours.

For my image of God the Holy Spirit, I turn to a young poet still in her twenties, Nancy McCready.

Start with my toes,
you old Ghost
Spirit the soles of my shoes
and teach me a Pentecostal
Boogaloo
Sprain my ankles with dancing
Sandle around my feet,
to roam with me in the rain
and feel at home in my footprints.

Oh! look at me spinning,
Sprinkling, tonguing, teaching,
Winsoming wondrous steps that
Lift me, how!
We'd better quit now,
too all dizzy down giggly
Stop - you're tickling me
(my funnybone's fickle for you)
Stop - I'll drop.
I'm dying, I'm flying.

With your winding my feet and
legs and waist
Lasooed
Stop chasing fool - I'm racing from you
Don't catch me
Do.
I'll drown
O! drown me
most
For I love you
so
You old Ghost![2]

---

[2]Nancy McCready, "Poem for Pentecost." Unpublished.

In its own way, Mrs. McCready's image is even more outrageous than Francis Thompson's. For God is not merely a bloodhound pursuing us without any thought of giving up the chase, he is a dancer inviting us to join a boogaloo with him. He is a whirling, swirling dervish trying to catch us up in the mad frenzy of his rhythm; an old Ghost who haunts us with an invitation to the dance.

I doubt very much whether the poet, an Irish Catholic from the South Side of Chicago, has ever wrestled with Friedrich Nietzsche, yet she shares with the bizarre German philosopher the conviction that a dancing God is the only God worth believing in. As Sam Keen says in his book, *To a Dancing God:* "The dancing God inhabits us as often in discipline as in spontaneity; as much in decision as in ecstasy; as frequently in promises as in immediacy."[3] Keen asserts that his dancing God is neither Apollo nor Dionysus but a combination of them both: "As always, the sacred shatters all the categories we necessarily use to understand the sacred. So the dance continues."[4]

And so the old Ghost continues to haunt us.

---

[3]Sam Keen, *To a Dancing God.* New York: Harper & Row, 1970, p. 5.

[4]*Ibid.*

Chapter One

THE NOTION OF GOD

IN THE Introduction I said that the issue is not whether or not there is a God, since every man has a God; the issue is, rather, who our God is. It is this restating of the question which seems to me is the principal contribution which social science can make to religious discussion. Social science realizes that every man must have a "meaning system," that is to say, a set of underlying convictions about the ultimate nature of reality. "The notion of God" is merely a convenient summary of this interpretive scheme or meaning system of ours. When man speaks of God, he is in fact asserting what his convictions are about ultimate reality. A man who says he "does not believe in God" is merely rejecting a set of convictions about ultimate reality which he links with the term "God." But he is also stating explicitly or implicitly his own ultimate concept of reality; whether or not he wishes to use the symbol of God he nonetheless has an image of ultimate reality every bit as much as does any other man. He who asserts that he "does not believe in God" is in fact asserting that he does not believe in certain other people's God and that he does not like to use the category, God, when describing his own ultimate cultural system. He is perfectly within his rights in choosing his own mode of expression and also in rejecting other people's interpretive schemes, but he misses the whole point if he thinks he has ended the discussion when he asserts that there is no God. If he wishes to continue the discussion, he is still under obligation to explicate his own interpretive scheme. If he does not want to call that interpretive scheme "God" that is all well and good, but he must not attempt to escape from the fact that the issue is interpretive schemes and not some great hangman in the sky or a senior vice president in charge of morale and happiness.

In his many writings on the subject, the distinguished anthropologist Clifford Geertz argues that a need for meaning systems is built into the human condition. As the only major animal lacking an elaborate system of instincts man depends upon his culture for survival. Geertz contends the evolution of human culture and the evolution of the human organism have gone hand in hand. It is only the development of culture (that is to say, man's collection of meaning systems) that has enabled the physical organism to evolve. His symbols, his meanings, his interpretations are, according to Geertz, "templates" by which man charts a path through the chaotic phenomena that impinge on his consciousness. Man without culture, man without meaning, is not simply a naked ape; he is, rather, a monstrous creature with no hope for survival – a biological misfit and disaster.

In Geertz's theoretical framework there are a number of different meaning systems with which man copes with the complexity of reality: science, common sense, ideology, history, art. But the ultimate in meaning systems is the religious one, precisely because religion addresses itself to the most basic questions that man must ask – that is to say, questions about the ultimate nature and structure of reality. Man must have a religious meaning system, according to Geertz, because neither science, nor common sense, nor any of his other cultural systems enables him to cope adequately with such problems as suffering, moral evil, death, or the unexpected. Such issues impinge not only on questions of interpretation but also on the

more basic question of the *interpretability* of reality. If man cannot cope with the problems that transcend science and common sense – with the ultimate
issues – then the whole interpretability of reality
threatens to come tumbling down upon him. Furthermore, his religious interpretive scheme not only describes for man what reality really is, it also tells
him how he ought to behave. World-view and ethos
are, in Geertz's framework, but different sides of the
same coin. World-view tells us what ultimate reality
is really like, and ethos tells us how the good man
ought to live in order to be in harmony with ultimate
reality. Nor is religion merely a set of symbols that
can cope with critical issues in life, because the uncanny and the unexpected occur every day, or almost
every day, and demand of us that we have recourse
to some interpretive scheme that underpins the whole
structure of our intellectual and moral reality.

Geertz – along with the other social scientists who
assume similar positions – is not asserting that all
men are "religious" in the sense of being "devout."
Rather he is asserting that all men need to a greater
or lesser extent some kind of cultural system that
enables them to cope with the ultimate questions of
what life is; whether the Really Real is good or bad;
whether good conquers evil, or evil, good; whether
life conquers death, or death, life; whether there is
any purpose in life; and how the good man ought to behave. Some men are more concerned about these
issues than others. At certain times in our lives the
issues are more pressing than at others. Some men
develop far more elaborate cultural systems than
others. Some men are more inclined to give lip ser-
vice to the "official" cultural system than others.
Atheists, agnostics, skeptics, and even hypocrites are,
according to Geertz, to be found in every society,
primitive or advanced. To state that man needs reli-

gion in the sense of an ultimate cultural system is not to say that man must necessarily postulate a transcendental validation of his interpretive scheme, though most men do and have. It is merely to assert that man must have a meaning system; or, to put the matter somewhat differently, man must have something to believe in; he must have a faith. The critical question in religious discussion, then, is not, is there a God? But, what is your faith? The God we describe is a symbol of how we interpret reality. When, therefore, one speaks as I do in this volume of the God of the Christians, one is necessarily and inevitably speaking of what Christians believe reality is all about; of how Christians answer the questions of whether life has purpose or not; whether good triumphs over evil, or evil over good; life over death, or death over life; and how man ought to live.

If you say to me, "I don't believe in God," I am afraid I don't know what you are talking about, and I am forced to ask you what you do believe in. If, on the other hand, you say, "I don't believe in your God," you mean that you do not believe in the Christian interpretation of reality, in Christianity as a cultural system, to use Geertz's category; and if you really know what the Christian interpretive scheme is (and a lot of people think they do and actually don't) and reject it, then of course that is your privilege. Though I feel sorry for you, I don't expect you to like my God; indeed, in many respects he is a rather difficult God to deal with – chasing us down the road like a hound dog and cavorting around us like an inebriated boogaloo dancer. No, he is not an easy God to cope with at all, and as I said in the introduction, he is a pushy, Jewish God; if you are anti-Semitic, that's your problem. Yes, indeed, it's up to you whether you like my God or not, but at least you should do me and him the honor of finding out who he is before you reject him.

There have been many different kinds of God men have worshiped, each one of which has represented a different world-view, and, in particular, a different solution to the question of good and evil.

Apparently, the first God man had was a "Sky God." Even though archaeology and anthropology have not found any societies where the Sky God exists by himself, they are still inclined to conclude that the Sun God, or the Moon God, or the God in the Skies probably antedates the multitude of lesser deities with whom he is surrounded in most of the nature religions of which we have actual knowledge. At least the nature religions themselves seem to attribute some kind of priority to the Sky God, and there is some reason to believe that the most primitive of food-gathering and hunting peoples are more concerned with the Sky God than are the more advanced of the pastoral and agricultural peoples.

The Sky God has much in common with the deistic god of the 17th and 18th century Enlightenment and the "Prime Mover" of Aristotelian metaphysics. In any of these three images, God is the one who set the mechanism in motion and then let it run by itself, to be periodically fouled up either by men in the deist and Aristotelian versions, or by the lesser gods and spirits in the nature religion version. The Sky God or the Great Architect of the Universe created the whole mess and then left it alone, presumably to busy himself about other things.

To the two critical religious questions, then, the Sky God image says that creation was somehow or another good, but that it has been corrupted either by the gods and the spirits or by men, and that ultimate reality is not accessible to men, but far removed from them and quite unconcerned about them.

The pastoral and agricultural peoples were necessarily deeply involved in the fertility process. The reproduction of plants and animals represented the most basic reality in their existence; hence, the powers of ultimate reality were seen at work in the fertility process, and large numbers of spirits, both good and evil, were seen as facilitating or threatening the smooth cycle of animal or plant fertility. Did the Nile rise too late or too soon? Then the proper gods had not been appeased. Did the rains come at the wrong time or not at all? Then the proper spirit has not been invoked. Was the harvest a poor one? Something had gone wrong with the gods' support of men.[1] In the nature religions, then, reality was seen as a complex of good and evil. There were good gods and bad gods, there was good reality and bad reality. The creator or the demiurge had merely pushed back the forces of evil and chaos somewhat and introduced some kind of order and system in the world. When man, through his rituals and through his tending of the fields and the flocks continued the work of ordering, he cooperated with the work of the demiurge. Nonetheless, the ordering of chaos was, at best, a precarious task.

In some of the archaic cultures, as in some primitive tribes, the deck is seen as stacked in favor of the forces of evil. Ultimate reality, then, is more evil than good, and God or the gods are conceived of as cantankerous, difficult, and surly individuals whom man must constantly placate lest the slightest violation

---

[1]It is not at all my intention to ridicule the nature religions. As a number of very astute observers such as Levi-Strauss, Eliade, Gilkey, Henri Frankfort, and Giorgio di Santillana have observed, primitive man's mythology was not merely superstition, it also was a highly elaborate scientific code for recording scientific insights which were no less important in human development because writing, or mathematics, or even abstract thought were not available to describe them.

of obligation or ritual bring the wrath of God upon them.

In other and more benign forms of nature religions reality is seen as striking a balance more in favor of good than of evil. But under such circumstances the gods or god, while benign, are also absent-minded. It is not so much required that man placate the gods as it is to constantly remind them of the promises they have made. If things go wrong it is not so much that the gods are angry, but that they have fallen asleep. In the nature religions, then, ultimate reality is seen as ambiguous, composed of both good and evil. The gods, quite accessible to man, are either to be pleaded with or placated. Let us not dismiss this imagery as being a creation of the primitive past, for many of us who pretend to be Christians in fact share a view of God not unlike that of the nature religions: he is either a cantankerous individual to be placated or a forgetful one to be harassed about the promises he has made. One simply has to read through the book of Psalms, for example, to see that the Jews, who had gone far beyond the simple fertility gods of their Semitic ancestors, spent a good deal of their time trying either to calm God down or to wake him up.

For the nature religions, then, ultimate reality was ambiguous, a mixture of good and evil. God was accessible and had to be dealt with through a form of collective bargaining, and salvation came through keeping some sort of peace and harmony in man's relationship with the gods.

The Greek image of God was far more sophisticated than that of their archaic predecessors, for the Greeks were far more sophisticated people, and their relationships with each other much more complicated than that of the simple peasants of the preceding centuries. In the world-view of Greek mythology the role of man was essentially a tragic one. Destiny, or fate, was rigorous and inflexible. The gods were capricious, arbitrary, and jealous beings who resented man's prideful attempts to raise himself to the state of a god. They also meddled indiscriminantly and selfishly in human affairs. Man was a plaything of the gods, and his tragic destiny was the result of his inability to escape from the whims of the gods. Saturn, the dim Sky God, was asleep somewhere, and unless he awoke (and there were only vague hopes that he would) the gods would not repent of their ways. Thus, for all the beauty of Greek poetry and drama, the Greeks ultimately had come down on the side of those nature religions which saw the gods - that is to say, reality - as more evil than good. In the Greek view of things, reality was tragic if not evil. The gods were accessible but to be avoided whenever possible, and salvation was out of the question.

However, there was another element of Greek thought represented by the Orphic myths and later by Plato who converted these myths into an elaborate philosophical system; a system which represented in Greek dress the immense human breakthrough also to be found in the world religions of Persia and India. Man's spirit was good but it was captured in a body which was evil. Salvation came through knowledge, that is to say, a kind of self-discipline that enabled one to break through the barriers of the flesh and contemplate the goodness and truth of the spirit. Man was, in fact, an emanation of God, and he would return to God to the extent that he could free himself from the folly and the passion of his body. In the Platonic religion (and its counterparts in the East) God becomes an Idea which man attempts to know; the reality of the spirit is good, the reality of the body is evil, and the Really Real is accessible through knowledge and contemplation. Man can find salvation by breaking away from the bonds of the flesh.

The Sky God, the Great Architect of the Universe,

the Supreme Idea, the Cantankerous Spirit, the Sleepy
Spirit, and Zeus and his carousing cronies on Olympus
all have one thing in common: man must pursue them if
he wishes to receive favors from them (though in the
case of Zeus and his crowd, one does one's best to stay
out of the way). The God of the Jews and, later, his
Christian son are another matter altogether. The question about them is not how man can gain access to them,
but whether it is at all possible for man to get away
from them. A number of famous characters, including
Jonah, tried and discovered that they should have
saved their breath.

The ancient Israelites were extremely simple no-
madic people, and their Yahweh was essentially a
Sky God, howling around them in the desert winds.
Unlike most of the Sky Gods, he did not choose to recede
into the background as the Jews became pastoral and
then peasant people; nor did he permit himself to be
pushed aside by the fertility spirits on the lands of
Canaan. There was a vigorous battle between Yahweh
and the fertility spirits, and at times the outcome was
touch and go, but Yahweh finally won. It was not so
much, as Walter Harrelson has pointed out, that the
fertility elements were eliminated from the Jewish religion. The feast of the Passover combines in the
Paschal lamb of the pastoral people and the unleavened
bread of the agricultural people two ancient fertility
ceremonies. But the ceremonies have been historicized.
They do not stand for spring fertility festivals. They
now stand for Yahweh's life-giving covenant with his
people. Fertility still exists and the Jews still depend
on it, but now, fertility is definitively subjected to Yahweh who blesses both the crops and the flocks. He is the
Sky God who did not go away. Unlike the Greek Saturn
he did not fall asleep.

But neither was he prepared to spend his time sitting
on Sinai fiercely issuing thunderbolts. He established a

"covenant" with his people; that is to say, he declared that they were his people and he was their God, almost whether they wanted it or not.

In the Jewish version of things, then, the ultimate reality is basically good. Evil comes through man's infidelity and sinfulness, salvation comes by returning to Yahweh, or, more specifically, by surrendering to his implacable love; and as for the Really Real being accessible, he is as accessible as a husband who is sexually aroused is accessible to his wife. If that image seems too strong, it must be emphasized that it is one that is inescapably present in both the Old and the New Testaments.

It will be seen that the Jewish "interpretive scheme" is by far the most hopeful of those described thus far in this chapter, for it asserts that not merely is reality ultimately good, but also that it is, one might almost say, aggressively good; good even when we don't want it to be, and good whether we like it that way or not.

There have been many variations on the basic interpretive schemes that we have described so far. In the Greek world, for example, there were two responses to the tragic situation in which man found himself. One was that of Apollo: a calm, rational, orderly, self-controlled life that accepted tragic destiny calmly and coolly and lived with dignity and self-possession in the face of tragedy. Roman Stoicism and much of contemporary Existentialism are merely historical adaptations of the Apollonian approach to tragedy. The alternative Greek response was that of Dionysus: one escaped the ugliness of tragedy by "tuning out" and "turning on"; by giving oneself over to the mystical and the orgiastic. In the dance, in the spirit of Bacchus, in ecstasy, in mystical rituals man found some release from the heavy burden of tragedy that was his lot.

The two principal secular religions of the modern world, scientism and Marxism, have their counterparts in the past. Marxism is an essentially "this-worldly" salvation religion complete with a chosen people (the proletariat), and eschatological future (Communist society), a fiery prophet (Karl Marx), a bible *(Das Capital* and the Communist *Manifesto),* and an absolute assurance of salvation (Dialectical Materialism). Salvation will come in the future in this most eschatological of world views, and even though the individual will not be able to enjoy it, at least he will have the privilege of knowing that he has helped to create it.

Scientism, on the other hand, is basically Stoic and Platonic, though it does have some salvationist strains about it. Man's destiny is ultimately tragic, but he can fend off the tragedy, at least for a time, by living the rational, intelligent life, and by creating the sober, orderly, liberal society. Salvation, such as it may be, comes through the increase of scientific knowledge and through the scientific ordering of human relationships.

At the present time, however, it seems that secular rationalism is shifting from an Apollonian to a Dionysian posture, signaled by Harvey Cox's migration from *The Secular City* to *The Feast of Fools.* The non-rational and the irrational, the orgiastic and the mythical dimensions of man have become popular once again in the liberal, intellectual world, and cognitive rationalism has been dethroned as a demiurge to be replaced if not by Dionysus then either by Pan or Bacchus. Rock music, drugs, encounter marathons, and even eschatological communes are seen as at least temporary salvation from man's tragic destiny.

There is, of course, one important and basic question that has to be asked about man's search for an interpretive scheme. Is it necessary for him to postulate some sort of Transcendental Reality which validates the explanation? Is the Really Real, which we symbolize by God, something which transcends the "this worldly," however deeply it may also be involved in the "this worldly?" If the question is so posed, one must respond by saying that at least on the explicit level, interpretive schemes need not assume a Transcendent unless, as in the Jewish and Christian interpretive schemes, religion takes an extraordinarily hopeful view of human destiny. In other words, some interpretive schemes require a Transcendent and others do not. The validity of the assumption of transcendence, of course, cannot be proven or disproven by rational or scientific argument. One *believes* in the Transcendent or in the non-Transcendent only through an act of faith. In either case, one must leap beyond the available empirical and rational data. It is not my intention in the present book to engage in an argument about plausibility of the Transcendent; I have done so in another volume;[2] and both Professors Langdon Gilkey and Peter Berger have written extensively on the issue.[3] For the purpose of the present volume I am assuming the Christian perspective. Instead of trying to convince my readers that the Really Real is, in the final analysis, totally benign, I intend to point out that that is the core of the Jewish and Christian message, and that if one is accepting or rejecting these two traditions, one should know what it is that one is accepting or rejecting; for Yahweh storming around the desert, Jesus walking the hills of Galilee, and Mrs. McCready's frolicking Ghost are all symbolic ways of representing the Ultimate in the Jewish and Christian tradition. Reality is Good; indeed much better than man dares to expect, or is even pre-

---

[2]Andrew M. Greeley, *Youth Wants to Know: Does God Still Speak?* Camden: Thomas Nelson, 1970.

[3]Langdon Gilkey, *Taming the Whirlwind.* Indianapolis: Bobbs Merrill, 1969. and Peter Berger, *Rumor of Angels.* New York: Doubleday, 1969.

pared to believe. The Semitic traditions proclaim good news, and man nervously responds by wondering if the good news is too good to be true.

It would be yielding to the peculiar arrogance of our time, which sees itself as dicovering for the first time problems which in fact have been part of the human condition for a millennium, to think that belief is any more difficult today than it has been in the past. We very superciliously think of ourselves as a superior breed, representing an inevitable development in the evolutionary process over the naive, superstitious ignoramuses who preceded us. We alone have discovered that faith is difficult. We alone have problems in accepting the Good News. We alone wonder whether there is a Transcendent or not. And yet faith is always difficult, for as Joseph Ratzinger puts it:

> . . . belief signifies the decision that at the very core of human existence there is a point which cannot be nourished and supported on the visible and tangible, which encounters and comes into contact with what cannot be seen and finds that it is necessary for its own existence.[4]

Faith for Ratzinger is a "con-version," a reversal, a turning around, a leaping beyond the physical. He adds:

> It is not just today, in the specific conditions of our modern situation, that belief or faith is problematical, indeed almost something that seems impossible, but that it has always meant a leap, a some-

---

[4]Joseph Ratzinger, *Introduction to Christianity*, trans. by J. R. Foster. New York: Herder and Herder, 1970, p. 24.

what less obvious and less easily recognizable one
perhaps, across an infinite gulf, a leap namely out
of the tangible world that presses on man from
every side. Belief has always had something of an
adventurous break or leap about it, because in every
age it represents the risky enterprise of accepting
what plainly cannot be seen as the truly real and
fundamental. Belief was never simply the attitude
obviously corresponding to the whole slant of human
life; it has always been a decision calling on the
depths of existence, a decision that in every age
demanded a turnabout by man that can only be
achieved by an effort of will.[5]

It requires, then, a leap of faith to decide that there
is some sort of transcendental validation of our meaning system. Man can, perhaps, do without the Transcendent, but it is much less clear that he can do without the sacred, for even the most "this worldly"
explanation of existence quickly takes on a sacred
aura. Marxism, or Scientism, or Liberal Humanism
are as sacred to those who believe in them as are the
more traditional religions to their believers. That
which is "ultimate" quickly becomes "other," something quite different from the ordinary and the everyday. While it is possible to have an "other" that is
not "totally other," it is extremely difficult. Marxism,
Scientism, and Humanism become almost transcendent
for their adherents despite themselves.
  The sacred is the "totally other" (or the *ganz
andere* as Rudolf Otto put it in his *Das Heilige*).
It is perceived as a reality that is both *tremendens
et fascinosum,* a reality which is both terrifying and
fascinating. The sacred has about it a feeling of the
"numinous," something awesome and uncanny. It is

---

[5]*Ibid.,* p. 25.

a "breaking through" of a world which is perceived as being, if not completely beyond the present world, at least totally different from it. The sacred is encountered with overwhelming force in mystical and ecstatic experiences, and with real but considerably less power in more ordinary experiences. The sacred presents itself through a hierophany; it "appears," sometimes, indeed, in response to our seeking, but frequently unasked, unexpected, and even unwanted.

It is in experiencing the sacred that man feels himself in unity with the life-giving forces of the universe and the Force which underpins all the other forces When he experiences the sacred man knows that he is in touch with the Really Real – that which underpins everything else.

Can man do without the sacred? Undoubtedly some men can, though there is no evidence that this is a result of evolutionary progress, or that more men can do without it now than at any time in the past. But the testimony of social scientists on the need for the sacred is well-nigh unanimous ever since Emile Durkheim said, "There will always be religion." Everett Cherrington Hughes, one of the greats in American sociology, sees the human life difficult without recourse to the sacred.

> Those who have the cure of souls--pastors and psychiatrists--can tell better than I what burdens break and what sicknesses ravage the souls of those who, in the name of self-reliance, emancipation, or progress, try to act as if there were no cycle of youth, maturity, old age and death; no rhythms of inner peach and conflict, of guilt and freedom from guilt, of grief and of the healing of its wound.[6]

[6]Everett C. Hughes, *Men and Their Work*. Chicago: University of Chicago Press, 1959, p. 17.

And Edward Shils thinks that men will need the sacred and the ritual (which is a sacred activity) as long as they are seriously concerned about the meaning of life.

> Ritual is a stereotype, symbolically concentrated expression of beliefs and sentiments regarding ultimate things. It is a way of renewing contact with ultimate things, of bringing more vividly to the mind through symbolic performances certain centrally important processes and norms . . . the importance of ritual in any large society lies in its expression of an intended commitment to the serious element of existence, to the vital powers and norms which it is thought should guide the understanding and conduct of life. . . . As long as the category of the "serious" remains in human life, there will be a profound impulse to acknowledge and express an appreciation of the "seriousness" which puts the individual into contact with words and actions of symbolic import.[7]

And Mircea Eliade sees the alleged capacity of some men to dispense with the sacred as being a second "fall" of man.

> From one point of view it could almost be said that in the case of those moderns who proclaim that they are nonreligious, religion and mythology are "eclipsed" in the darkness of their unconscious - which means too that in such men the possibility of reintegrating a religious vision of life lies at a great depth. Or, from the Christian point of view, it could also be said that nonreligion is

---

[7]Edward Shils, "Ritual and Crisis," *The Religious Situation: 1969*, ed. Donald R. Cutler. Boston: Beacon Press, 1969, pp. 746-47.

equivalent to a new "fall" of man – in other words,
that nonreligious man has lost the capacity to live
religion consciously, and hence to understand and
assume it; but that, in his deepest being, he still
retains a memory of it, as, after the first "fall,"
the religious sense descended to the level of the
"divided consciousness"; now, after the second,
it has fallen even further, into the depths of the
unconscious; it has been "forgotten."[8]

One of the most frequently heard arguments of contemporary secularists is that man no longer "needs"
God, for man has now "come of age." He understands
what causes storms and why the sun moves across the
heavens between the equinoxes. He understands why
some constellations of stars slowly disappear from
the sky. He knows the origins of earthquakes, vol-
canoes, and hurricanes. He can control much sick-
ness and postpone death. The areas of "bafflement"
have declined, and therefore man no longer needs
either God or the ultimate interpretive scheme that
God symbolizes.

Two responses can quickly be made to such an
assertion:

1. While man can explain the movements of the
heavens and the activities of nature, more or less,[9]
and hence it can be said that absolutely speaking
the areas of bafflement in the natural world have declined. It does not follow that the primordial baffle-

---

[8]Mircea Eliade, *The Sacred and the Profane,* trans.
Willard R. Trask. New York: Harcourt, Brace and
Company, 1959, p. 213.

[9]Most of us really don't understand astrophysics,
nuclear physics, or theoretical physics, but we pre-
sume we can understand what goes on in the universe
because there are some scientists who can understand these three arcane disciplines.

ment over the phenomenon of human existence has changed in the slightest since the Ice Age. Man is still puzzled by the fact that he exists and baffled by the question of what is his destiny. The critical issues of life and death, good and evil, happiness and suffering have not been solved by scientific progress; and, in the nature of things, cannot be solved by such progress. Science and technology have increased man's knowledge and power. They have taken the mysteries out of many of the forces of nature (though at a price of causing us to lose our respect for nature and producing pollution), but they have not and cannot by themselves tell man whether Reality is gracious or malign, or some combination of both, and how he ought to live if he wishes to have a good life and obtain salvation.

2. If the areas of bafflement in the natural universe have declined, bafflement in the human and the interpersonal world has increased. Man's possibilities for growth and self-fulfillment are much greater than they have ever been before, and man's relationships with his fellows are much more complex than they ever were before. The quest for self fulfillment, for meaningful relationships produces areas of bafflement of which our Stone Age ancestors could not have dreamed. The mysteries of human relationships and of the human personality have grown more puzzling and complicated; hence generate a more intense demand for an interpretive scheme that will give man some idea of what direction his self fulfillment ought to take, and what norms ought to regulate his relationships with his fellows. The mysteries of the physical world may have declined somewhat; the mysteries of the psychological and interpersonal world, however, have increased. For all his scientific knowledge and technological skills, contemporary man is, if anything, even more "baffled" than his predecessors.

To summarize this chapter, God is a symbol of man's interpretive scheme - his meaning system. God represents that conviction about the ultimate nature of reality. He who wishes to reject the symbols of God is still obliged to propose his own interpretive scheme; for without an interpretive scheme that answers the ultimate questions most men cannot lead a human life. Absolutely speaking, the interpretive scheme need not postulate something that transcends this world, but there seems to be a strong built-in strain for any interpretive scheme to become quasi-transcendental. That which we believe in, that which has become our faith becomes sacred for us, because even if we argue that it is only "this worldly," it still, as Clifford Geertz says, possesses, "an aura of unique factuality." If it is not exactly "totally other," it comes very close to converting itself into the "totally other," even if we do not want it to. That which man believes becomes numinous; it represents a reality that is somehow beyond himself - both terrifying and fascinating. Social scientists observe that man has always had a God, a religion, and the sacred; and that, indeed, these are generally the same things. It also very much doubts whether man will ever be able to dispense with God, religion, and the sacred. The bizarre resurgency of witchcraft, divination, astrology, mysticism, and religious communes among the protesting young of our day is ample proof, if we needed it, that the secular, rationalist, scientific materialism of the American intellectual community is simply not enough for man to live by.

Chapter Two

THE RESURRECTION OF MYTHS

I T MIGHT be argued at this point that I have, in effect, done away with God by "reducing" him to the state of a symbol. If all God does is to act as a symbolic representation of our interpretive scheme, then we might just as well dispense with the symbol and state the interpretive scheme without cluttering it up with the obsolescent notion of a God. Interpretive schemes may be fine, but the figure of God is obviously mythological.

Such an argument, which I suspect is quite wide-spread in contemporary American Catholicism, demonstrates how much our society has been permeated by the assumption of positive science: only that which can be stated quantitatively and abstractly is "real." This assumption, which is being rapidly abandoned in many parts of the scientific community (and was never accepted by many of the great philosophers of science like Michael Polanyi), has somehow or other seeped down into the collective unconsciousness of many Americans, probably through the inferior educations that we have all received. But as soon as someone asks if God is "only symbolic" or "only mythological," that person has displayed a profound ignorance both about the complexity of human knowledge and the indispensable role of myth and symbol in human life. Symbol and myth are not any less true than abstract and rationalistic statement. Quite the contrary, they might even claim to be more true, because they try to grapple with more of reality than the abstract scientific proposition. They are a different kind of language representing a different form

38

of knowledge, but not, let it be insisted, by any means
an inferior form of knowledge. Let us turn to Dr. John
Schaar, an outspoken member of the New Left, for an
analysis of the inadequacies of scientific abstraction
as the only form of human knowledge and the indispensable role of symbol and myth in human knowledge,
life, and organization.

The language in which the knowledge appropriate
to humanly significant leadership is expressed is
also very different from the language of rational
and objective discourse. It is a language profuse
in illustration and anecdote, and rich in metaphor
whose sources are the human body and the dramas
of action and responsibility. This language is sug-
gestive and alluring, pregnant, evocative – in all
ways the opposite of the linear, constricted, jar-
gonized discourse which is the ideal of objective
communication. Decisions and recommendations
are often expressed in parables and visions whose
meanings are hidden to outsiders but translucent
to those who have eyes to see. Teaching in this
language is done mainly by story, example, and
metaphor – modes of discourse which can probe
depths of personal being inaccessible to objective
and managerial discourse. Compare the Sermon on
the Mount with the latest communique from the Of-
fice of Economic Opportunity in the War on Pover-
ty; or Lincoln's Second Inaugural with Nixon's
first.[1]

Chemistry, physics, biology, even to some extent the
social sciences and the humanities, may be appropriate areas for the use of language which has had all its

[1]John Schaar, "Reflections on Authority," *New
American Review*, Vol. 8, 1970, pp. 77-78.

poetic and imaginative content filtered out; but the scholarly disciplines are not the whole of human life – not by a long shot – and the language and cognition appropriate for the scholarly disciplines cannot deal with love, with hope, with faith, or with ultimate realities. When man wishes to speak of these things he uses symbols: songs, dances, poems, drama, and stories. The myth is nothing more than a story (which may be converted into song, dance, and drama) by which man tries to cope with the Ultimate Reality. The myth is a story through which he attempts to incarnate in richly allusive and symbolic language appealing to the total human personality the interpretive scheme by which he lives. They myth-maker is not interested in writing scientific history, in telling all the factual details; he is rather trying to tell it like it *really* is, and he arranges the details to make as clear as possible to the listener the nature of the reality he is trying to convey. In American political life, for example, we have myths of the great leaders and the great events: George Washington, the Father of our Country, the Moses figure who led us out of tyranny into a new land of freedom; Abraham Lincoln, the Christ figure, who freed the slaves and brought us through a terrible, bloody crisis to a new unity and gave his life in the process; John Kennedy, the young knight of the Round Table, struck down by blind and irrational forces at the height of his promise. All of these are mythological figures.[2]

---

[2]Even the most rational, realistic, and scientific among us have our own myths. Thus, for example, there is the myth of Senator Joseph McCarthy who created, it is alleged, a "reign of terror" in the American university in the early 1950s; or, in somewhat different mythological language, he led a "witch hunt." In strict historical fact, McCarthy's victims in the university were a very small handfull, but the

Scientific historians will argue that Washington was a sometimes bumbling, frequently lazy, and occasionally very undependable Virginia aristocrat; and Abraham Lincoln was a crude backwoods politician with a fondness for telling very dubious stories; and that John Kennedy was one of the shrewdest and most ruthless political operators that the American Irish have ever produced. Which version is more "true?" Such a question is obviously unanswerable. There are different kinds of truth, because there are different kinds of knowledge and language games. The scientific historian is trying to compile detailed, concrete, documentable facts. The mythologist is trying to capture the spirit, the atmosphere, the meaning, the ultimate reality of a particular time in history. He is not really interested, at least not as a mythologist, in precise historical accuracy. If we tell him that Abraham Lincoln was coarse and vulgar, the mythologist shrugs his shoulders and says, in effect, "So what? He still lead us through the Civil War and held the Union together, and that's what I'm interested in." If we tell the mythologist about all the failings of George Washington, he can still respond by saying, "But he was, after all,

---

myth is not thereby false, for it is an attempt to tell in story form about the very anxious and troubled times in the late 1940s and early 1950s when Americans discovered that the great victory of World War II was a hollow one. Similarly, there has already evolved a mythology about the Chicago conspiracy trial. One New York liberal assured me that Judge Hoffman was the most corrupt judge who ever bought a judgeship from Mayor Daley. I pointed out that Judge Hoffman was appointed by Dwight Eisenhower before Richard Daley became mayor of Chicago, but my friend was not at all chagrined by this information. The factual details were not important. What was important was the symbolic interpretation of what he took to be the repressive situation in which American dissenters found themselves.

the leader of the Continental Armies and the first president of our nation." And we don't even have to be told at the present time that it was not so much the specific details of John Kennedy's personality, but the great ideas which he symbolized that have made him within a decade of his death a man of immense symbolic importance all around the world.

Does one know more or less about Abraham Lincoln after one has gone through Sandburg's multi-volume work? One surely knows more about the concrete historical facts of his life, but if in the process of reading Lincoln's biography one loses touch with the meaning of Lincoln the symbol, one may, in fact, know less about the total reality of the man's role in American history.

The myth-maker, then, is telling a story to make a point. We may not happen to agree with his point, but at least we should hear him out instead of quarreling with the factual details. For it is the point with which he is concerned and not the factual details.

Let us imagine, for example, that we are recounting to a friend the story of either a quarrel with someone else or an automobile accident. We will not, I think, be terribly concerned in either instance with listing precisely the chronological order of events or quoting exactly the words that were said, for we know that if we get bogged down in such details the "point" of the incident is going to be obscured. What we will relate to our friend, rather, is a summary of the event arranged in such a way that we communicate to him our interpretation of what happened. Some details will be omitted, others will be emphasized, and still others may even be modified somewhat in the interest of making clear our explanation and interpretation of what transpired. We are, in other words, telling a story to communicate an interpretation; we are engaging in myth-making. Whether someone interrupts us to modify a quotation or to suggest that we have got the chronology slightly wrong or some of the details are confused, we are likely to become highly irate. Chronology and details may be important in a court of law or even to someone who is writing a dissertation on our experience, but they are not all that pertinent save as they fit in our explanation of what *really* happened.

By now the reader has either discovered the difference between mythological and symbolic discourse on the one hand and positive, scientific discourse on the other, and has agreed that the mythological is valid, or I shall never be able to persuade him by further examples.

But let us hear what four scholars of myth have to say on the subject. Professor Alan Watts describes a myth as, "a complex story, some no doubt fact and some fantasy, which for various reasons human beings regard as demonstrations of the inner meaning of the universe and of human life." According to Watts, the "meaning is divined rather than defined, implicit rather than explicit, suggested rather than stated." He adds, "the language of myth and poetry is integrative, for the language of image is organic language . . . the mythological image is what gives sense and organization to experience."[3]

Professor Charles Long argues: "Myth . . . points to the definite manner in which the world is available for man. The word and contents of myth are of power." Myth integrates man's total life experience and interprets it for him; they go both higher and lower than scientific propositions.

---

[3]Alan Watts, *The Two Hands of God*. New York: George Braziller, 1963, p. 2.

A great deal of our modern cultural life presupposes the equation of literalness = truth. To some degree this is dictated by the scientific technological character of our culture, but we would find it difficult to believe that anyone in our culture lives entirely in a world of literal meanings. There are human experiences on the personal and cultural levels which can only be expressed in symbolic forms. These meanings are in many cases the most profound meanings in our personal and cultural lives. They are profound because they symbolize the specificity of our human situation – they make clear to us how the world exists for us and point up the resources and tensions which are present in our situation.[4]

Although one is not willing to put a dichotomy between the mythic and the scientific:

The presence of the type of thought which we call scientific is too pervasive in our contemporary life to justify such an alternative. We do not, however, interpret this to mean that the mythic as a structure of human awareness is no longer operative in our age. Rather, it presents to us the problem of dealing with the fundamental relatedness of the mythic and the scientific. One mode cannot replace the other; the generalizing method of scientific thought cannot do justice to the life of man as he experiences it, and the mythic mode of apprehension cannot remain so specific and concrete that it becomes esoteric or subjective.[5]

Mircea Eliade, the greatest of the students of what used to be called comparative religion and is now called "history of religions" observes, "What we

---

[4]Charles Long, *Myths of Creation*. New York: George Braziller.

[5]*Ibid.*

may call symbolic thought makes it possible for man to move freely from one level of reality to another. Indeed, 'to move freely' is an understatement: symbols . . . identify, assimilate, and unify diverse levels and realities that are to all appearances incompatible."[6]

Eliade sees the myth as integrating man not only with the rest of the universe but also with himself, and argues that such integration makes possible a "wholeness" in human life that is impossible for man who attempts to suppress his mytho-poetic inclinations.

> Man no longer feels himself to be an "air-tight" fragment, but a living cosmos open to all the other living cosmoses by which he is surrounded. The experiences of the world at large are no longer something outside him and therefore ultimately "foreign" and "objective"; they do not alienate him from himself but, on the contrary, lead him toward himself, and reveal to him his own existence and his own destiny. The cosmic myths and the whole world of ritual thus appear as existential experiences to primitive man: he does not lose himself, he does not forget his own existence when he fulfills a myth or takes part in a ritual; quite the reverse; he finds himself and comes to understand himself, because those myths and rituals express cosmic realities which ultimately he is aware of as realities in his own being. To primitive man, every level of reality is so completely open to him that the emotion he felt at merely seeing anything as magnificent as the starry sky would have been as strong as the most "intimist" personal experience felt by a modern. For, thanks chiefly to his symbols, the real existence of primitive man was not the broken and alienated existence lived by civilized man today.[7]

---

[6]Mircea Eliade, *Patterns in Comparative Religion.* New York: Sheed and Ward, 1958, p. 455.

[7]*Ibid.* pp. 455-456.

Eliade argues that the myth is a paradigm, a primordial event which took place in "real" time. What happened since the myth is simply a reflection of that myth. The gods *ordered* the universe. Man's reenactment of the myth is his participation in and reflection of that act of ordering.

The myth relates a sacred history, that is, a primordial event that took place at the beginning of time, *ab initio*. But to relate a sacred history is equivalent to revealing a mystery. For the persons of the myth are not human beings; they are gods or culture heroes, and for this reason their *gesta* constitute mysteries; man could not know their acts if they were not revealed to him. They myth, then, is the history of what took place *in illo tempore,* the recital of what the gods or the semidivine beings did at the beginning of time. To tell a myth is to proclaim what happened *ab origine*. Once told, that is, revealed, the myth becomes apodictic truth; it establishes a truth that is absolute. 'It is so because it is said that it is so,' the Netsilik Eskimos declare to justify the vaildity of their sacred history and religious traditions. The myth proclaims the appearance of a new cosmic situation or of a primordial event. Hence it is always the recital of a creation; it tells how something was accomplished, began to *be*. It is for this reason that myth is bound up with ontology; it speaks only of *realities,* of what *really* happened, of what was fully manifested.[8]

The myth, then, brings mankind into contact with the *real*. It enables him to transcend the phenomenal world of confusion and threatening chaos in which he lives and break through to the ordering by which chaos

---

[8]Mircea Eliade, *The Sacred and the Profane*. New York: Harcourt, Brace and Company, 1957, p. 95.

was first defeated and continues to be restrained.

This faithful repetition of divine models has a two-fold result:(1) by imitating the gods, man remains in the sacred, hence in reality; (2) by the continuous reactualization of paradigmatic divine gestures, the world is sanctified. Men's religious behavior contributes to maintaining the sanctity of the world.[9]

Henri Frankfort in *Before Philosophy* insists that:

. . . the imagery of myths is therefore by no means allegory. It is nothing less than a carefully chosen cloak for abstract thought. The imagery is inseparable from the thought. It represents the form in which the experience has become conscious.[10]

And he goes on to say:

Myth is a form of poetry which transcends poetry in that it proclaims a truth; a form of reasoning which transcends reasoning in that it wants to bring about the truth it proclaims; a form of action, of ritual behaviour, which does not find its fulfillment in the act but must proclaim and elaborate a poetic form of truth.[11]

In other words, myth is truth told not abstractly but concretely. The myth-maker may be a poet but he is not a superstitious fool; he has chosen to grapple with reality with a story rather than a schematic proposition. Frankfort explains the difference between how the Babylonians would react to a rain storm and

---

[9]*Ibid.* p. 99.

[10]Henri Frankfort, Mrs. H. A. Frankfort, John A. Wilson, Thorkild Jacobsen, *Before Philosophy.* Middlesex: Penguin Books Ltd., paperback, 1946, p. 99. *Kingship and the Gods,* original title published by University of Chicago Press, ©1948.

[11]*Ibid.*

the way we would react:

> We would explain, for instance, that certain atmospheric changes broke a drought and brought about rain. The Babylonians observed the same facts but experienced them as the intervention of the gigantic bird Imdugud which came to their rescue. It covered the sky with the black storm clouds of its wings and devoured the Bull of Heaven, whose hot breath had scorched the crops.

> In telling such a myth, the ancients did not intend to provide entertainment. Neither did they seek, in a detached way and without ulterior motives, for intelligible explanations of the natural phenomena. They were recounting events in which they were involved to the extent of their very existence. They experienced, directly, a conflict of powers, one hostile to the harvest upon which they depended, the other frightening but beneficial: the thunderstorm reprieved them in the nick of time by defeating and utterly destroying the drought. The images had already become traditional at the time when we meet them in art and literature, but originally they must have been seen in the revelation which the experiences entailed. They are products of imagination, but they are not mere fantasy. It is essential that true myth be distinguished from legend, saga, fable, and fairy tale. All these may retain elements of the myth. And it may also happen that a baroque or frivolous imagination elaborates myths until they become mere stories. But true myth presents its images and its imaginary actors, not with the playfulness of fantasy, but with a compelling authority. It perpetuates the revelation of a "Thou."[12]

---

[12]*Ibid.* p. 15.

Frankfort like most contemporary scholars rejects
the notion that primitive man was somehow or other
"pre-logical." The ancients were aware as we are of
the linkage between cause and effect, but:

> Our view of causality, then, would not satisfy primi-
> tive man, because of the impersonal character of
> its explanations. It would not satisfy him, more-
> over, because of its generality. We understand phe-
> nomena, not by what makes them peculiar, but by
> what makes them manifestations of general laws.
> But a general law cannot do justice to the individual
> character of each event. And the individual character
> of the event is precisely what early man experiences
> most strongly.[13]

Myths, then, are true stories, not in the sense of
scientifically accurate descriptions, but rather in that
they are interpretations of reality cloaked in the language of the whole man and directed at the consciousness of the whole man. The neat, positivistic language
of empirical science is useless for coping with the
ultimate, the sacred, the transcendent. Man, therefore, turns to mythopoetic language and mythopoetic
knowledge. It is with this sort of language and this
sort of knowledge that he describes the relationships
between God - that is to say, the Really Real - and
man.[14] But the lurking positivist in each of us still
asks a gnawing question: granted that the myths describe the Really Real as personified in God, does that
mean that the myth-maker *really* thinks that there

---

[13]*Ibid.* pp. 24-25.

[14]In his book, *Religion and the Future of Science,*
Langdon Gilkey describes at considerable length how
even science has its own myths. In the absence of a
mythological structure of its own, even that most rationalistic of activities would not be able to operate.

is someone *out there?* The answer is that in his own level of thought and discourse the myth-maker certainly believes that there is someone out there, but he does not believe that the someone is a person in the same limited sense that we use the word in speaking of fellow human beings. What the myth-maker is trying to convey – at least if he is a Jewish or a Christian myth-maker – is that the Really Real does indeed care about us; far more in fact than we can possibly care about him. The myth-maker is saying not only that Ultimate Reality is good, but that it is benign and gracious; or as one theologian put it in the convoluted language that theologians use so as not to offend students who have had a course in introductory physics, "It would be wrong to deny to Ultimate Reality the highest attributes that we recognized in human persons."

But what the myth-maker is trying to convey to those who listen to his story can be stated with considerably more bluntness: Ultimate Reality is a Thou. One need not believe this, of course. Whether one believes it or rejects it, in either event, one must make a leap of faith. But this assertion is, nevertheless, at the very core of the Jewish and Christian religious traditions. The Really Real is a Thou, and a Thou who cares. If, gentle readers, you are going to reject the Christian mythology, make sure that you know what you are rejecting, because that is what the ball game is all about.

One of the most difficult and tiresome tasks for anyone who is attempting to expound the Christian message is the refusal of many men and women to go beyond quibbling over the details of the myth to face up to the reality that the myth is trying to convey.[15] Let

---

[15]Back in the days when book censorship was still taken seriously by the Catholic Church, one other-

us take two of the more important Christian myths, the Eucharistic supper and the resurrection, as examples. The basic theme of the Last Supper mythology is, of course, that the Church is a community of friends; that Jesus is present as a friend and that friendship exists among Christians and between Christians and Jesus when they gather around the table to eat the Eucharistic banquet – the banquet which continues Jesus's work in time and space. There can be no doubt that the very earliest Christians as reported in the New Testament firmly believed that Jesus was indeed really present in the Eucharistic meal. But a vast amount of energy has been expended on explaining and debating and agonizing over the precise nature of this presence of Jesus. I do not wish to minimize the importance of theological analysis, but I simply want to make the point that it is of much less importance to be able to explain "how" the real presence occurs than it is to be able to explain what it means; yet, most of our catechetical and theological effort, particularly in the last four or five centuries, seems to have fixated on the "how" to the deemphasizing if not the complete ignoring of the "what." One can only suspect that Jesus must be somewhat chagrined. People are so busy arguing about how the Eucharist happens that they seem to have lost interest in what it means; quite possibly because what it means is so frightening.

Similarly, the obvious theme of the resurrection myth is that mankind will live; that human life will triumph over death. But much of the concern of apol-

---

wise very helpful censor suggested that in a passage where I referred to Christian myths I put in a footnote asserting that I did not thereby intend to say that Christian teachings were false. Once again, we see an example of the pervasive modern assumption that myth, poetry, and symbol somehow aren't really true.

ogetic and catechetic effort has been not to attempt to
interpret and explain this fantastic conviction, but
rather to develop a theory of how exactly the resurrection happened; to harmonize the various accounts
in the four Gospels, and to provide satisfactory explanation to those who are worried about all the physical details. Such efforts are not an utter waste of time,
but they are in the final analysis rather beside the
point. In the words of Carl Braaten:

> In affirming the event of the resurrection, we are
> not offering a theory to explain it. What is basic to
> the Christian hope is that it happened and what it
> means, not how it happened. The urge to explain it,
> however, will never subside. Explanation is a dimen-
> sion of understanding we always seek. Nevertheless,
> it would be foolish to hold that an explanation is
> needed to gain access to the life it promises. That
> would be like refusing to watch television until one
> could explain electricity, or refusing to admit one
> had fallen in love before explaining how it happened.[16]

Braaten is not saying, and neither am I, that it is unimportant whether Jesus rose from the dead or not;
it is extremely important. What is more important
about the resurrection of Jesus is that it represents a
promise of life for all men, and what is relatively unimportant is the theory we devise to explain how the
resurrection occurred.

The catechetics and the apologetics of our collective
unconscious are so powerful, however, that it takes
some wrenching for us to view things from such a perspective. Yet, when some bright young radical theo-

---

[16]Carl E. Braaten, *The Future of God*. New York:
Harper & Row, 1969, p. 75. ©1969 by Carl E. Braaten.

logian announces that he no longer accepts the resurrection of Christ (and even suggests that the Apostles might really have stolen the body) we must shake our heads in dismay and assert that the bright young radical theologian has quite completely missed the point of the resurrection mythology. For the ultimate issue is whether man through Christ will triumph over death, whether the entire human race will triumph over death; for this is what the Christian message really says. If you are going to reject Christianity you may as well reject it because of its most outlandish claim, for it is much more difficult to believe that the whole race will conquer death than to believe that one man conquered death.

In other words, if one puts together the themes of the Eucharist and the resurrection and tries to find their meaning, one is forced to conclude the Christian interpretive scheme is saying that not only is the Really Real a Thou, but it is a Thou which came to us in order to assure us not merely that we could be friends, not merely that we could triumph over death, but that he would remain present among us to reinforce our friendship and to assure the triumph over death. This is, as I have said before, an outrageous and outlandish claim, but it is at the very center of the Christian interpretive scheme. If Christianity and its God are to be accepted or rejected, let them be so on those grounds and not on more trivial ones.

In most stages of human history the myths were enough; men accepted the mythological stories not as scientific and historical descriptions (for they did not know what scientific and historical descriptions were) but as explanations of the Real. In our era, however, because of the immense progress we have made in abstract thought and scientific understanding,[17] it is not enough merely to listen to the myths as others recount them. Before the total personality can accept the mythological narrative one must ask, what does it mean? It is therefore necessary in our age that myths be *interpreted.* Such interpretation does not mean that the myth is abandoned, but it does mean that we are explicitly aware of the rational and cognitive component of the myth. I would argue that this is the primary purpose of religious instruction at the present time. We ought not to be in the business of defending our myths. We simply ought to be explaining them so that those who accept them or reject them will know what they really are accepting or rejecting, and so those who wish to live by them will know the staggering richness of that by which they are living. I would like to view this volume as an exercise in such myth interpretation, even though I have had to devote the first half of it to clearing the ground away by explaining what myth is. The rest of the book will be devoted to an interpretation of the Christian mythology about God; that is to say, an explanation of what the Christian interpretive scheme is, and what are the answers to the basic issues which are conveyed by the Christian notion of God. As I have said before, I will be pleased if you like my God, but if you don't like him, at least be sure you don't like him for the right reasons.

For the Christian, it might be noted, the question of whether it is legitimate to use mythological and anthropomorphic categories in dealing with God has long since

---

[17]And let it be clear that I am not in any sense criticizing this progress. I am not one of those romanticists who reject scientific society. I am merely asserting that scientific knowledge and language cannot cope with the whole of human reality.

been settled because God Himself chose to do so. There is no one who is more anthropomorphic than our God, for he chose to become a man; not merely so that we could talk about him in anthropomorphic terms, but also, marvel of marvels, so that he could speak about himself in such terms. And when you stop to think about it, that's a pretty outlandish idea, too.

Chapter Three

THE FATHER

T HE OLD TESTAMENT is filled with splendid images of the Father: there is the Spirit brooding over the waters, Elohim walking in the garden with Adam in the cool of the day, the Guest visiting Abraham in his house, the angel wrestling with Jacob, the fiery desert warrior riding into battle with the Israelite troops, the burning bush, the pillar of cloud by day and the pillar of fire by night charting the way through the wilderness, the Middle Eastern chieftain sitting in his tent with his barons, discussing philosophical problems, as in Job, the blazing seraphim in Isaiah. But this is not to be a book about the whole of the Jewish and Christian symbol system. I wish to choose four images from the Old Testament and comment on them at some length.

The first image is of God the Covenanter. In the book of Joshua there is a splendid passage in which Joshua calls the people together and says that it probably wouldn't be a very good idea for them to be God's people. God is apt to be very vigorous and demanding, and he, Joshua, personally would not recommend that the people get involved in a deal with God. But the people become very insistent saying, after all, they don't have any other God, and they wouldn't know where to go if Yahweh was not their God. Joshua shakes his head in disagreement. He knows, and so do the rest of them, what kind of a God this is, and he simply cannot be responsible for what is going to happen to them if they accept God's pledge to be their God and also accept his definition of them as his people.

But the Israelites grow all the more insistent. Yahweh is, after all, not merely the only God they have but the best God they could find. They simply will not be put off. Yahweh has made his promise to be their God, and they are going to hold him to it.

Joshua has, of course, played the game very shrewdly. Perhaps having learned a lesson from the unhappy troubles his predecessor had, he has maneuvered the people into demanding something which they might have been very reluctant to accept if he had offered it to them. But both Joshua and the people know that in the final analysis they don't really have much choice. Yahweh has already made up his mind. He *is* their God and they *are* his people. He doesn't want sacrifices of them. He is even more weary of the hardness of the people's hearts and their blind assumption that sacrifices and burnt offerings can hide it. What Yahweh wants is them – their love, their devotion, their fidelity. Like Gideon's image of God which we presented in the Introduction, Yahweh is so determined to have them as his people that he can't help himself. They are stuck with him, but in a paradoxical way he is stuck with them.

The history of Israel, then, is a record of Yahweh's pursuit of his people. They periodically turn away from him either to worship false idols (to engage in the Canaanite fertility cults) or to put their reliance and faith in human power and human arms. In all instances they get themselves soundly thrashed by the Assyrians, the Babylonians, the Egyptians, or other marauding invaders, and come crawling back to Yahweh with a combination of sorrow because they had turned away from him and sulkiness because he had not protected them from their enemies. The prophets appear on the scene periodically to announce that Yahweh is upset, that the people are unfaithful, that they are turning away from the covenant he has made with them, and if they don't abandon their infidelity he will have no choice but to deliver them over to the hands of Cyrus (or Nebuchadnezzar or others of those rather bizarre warriors who came sweeping down out of the north). The prophets demand repentance and conversion. They insist that the people recognize the nature of their relationship with Yahweh and stop trying to escape it. But never, never at any point, is there the slightest hint that Yahweh is going to back down from his part of the bargain. He may have grown incredibly weary of his people, but he will not turn away from them.

There is a good deal of fierceness in this jealous old peasant warrior sitting up on the top of Sinai and growing wrathful over the infidelity of his people. But one misses the whole point of Yahweh the Covenanter if one thinks of the image as of someone who has lost his temper or is angry because people have broken the rules. Yahweh is jealous, perhaps, but it is a jealousy based on love.

We are so familiar with the Old Testament mythology that we do not realize how revolutionary it is; for Yahweh the Covenanter represents an extraordinary religious development. Other religions, indeed, know of incarnations, of God becoming involved in human affairs; but these involvements always occur in mythological time, a time before our present times and different from it. (According to some scholars, much mythology is cosmology, and the time in which gods become involved is the time that occurs in the stars and not on earth. One scholar even suggests that the flood tradition, which is almost universal in human religions, represents a flood not on earth but in the heavens.) But Yahweh intervenes not in mythological time but in historical time. The covenant he made on Sinai took place on a definite spot with a definite people in a more or less definite historical epoch. God was no longer sitting in his heavens watching things that happen on earth, or perhaps ignoring them. He had now chosen to come down to earth and get himself involved – involved in a permanent and definitive way. He committed himself to a people irrevocably and without qualification. It was as though God had decided that since man could not deal with him on his own plane, then he would come down and deal with man on man's plane. Or as one theologian has pointed out to me, if we say that it is man's sin to want to be like God, then God, too, sinned when he decided to become like man in order that he might engage in communication and affection with his creature. Not only was the covenanting God a revolutionary, he was a gambler. To become involved with men meant that he ran the risk of being rejected by them, even of their trying to kill him. The covenanting Yahweh is Yahweh taking a definitive step towards man: a step which in the Christian viewpoint was in anticipation of a much more dramatic step that still lay in the future.

Thus the underlying theme of the Yahweh as Covenanter myth is that the Really Real is not only a Thou, not only a Thou who cares, but a Thou who cares enough to become involved; and a Thou who will not be turned around no matter how often he is rejected.

The second symbolic image is of Yahweh the Liberator. The most important part of the convenant of Yahweh with his people is his commitment to lead them out of slavery and into a new life of freedom, a commitment made in Egypt even before Sinai and periodically repeated. The experience of Yahweh as liberator is the most fundamental component of the Jewish religious experience. It is Exodus, not Genesis, which is the fundamental book of the Old Testament. One very ancient statement of that myth is recorded in the book of Deuteronomy.

Then, in the sight of Yahweh your God, you must make this pronouncement: 'My father was a wandering Aramaean. He went down into Egypt to find refuge there, few in numbers; but there he became a nation, great, mighty, and strong. The Egyptians illtreated us, they gave us no peace and inflicted harsh slavery on us. But we called on Yahweh the God of our fathers. Yahweh heard our voice and saw our misery, our toil and our oppression; and Yahweh brought us out of Egypt with mighty hand and outstretched arm, with great terror, and with signs and wonders. He brought us here and gave us this land, a land where milk and honey flow.'[1]

The exodus myth, like the other central Israelite myths, is repeated in the Christian tradition. It represents the basic conviction of the Jewish and Christian traditions that Ultimate Reality is not only favorably disposed towards mankind but had committed itself to leading mankind out of slavery and into a new life. The covenant then is not merely a static commitment but a directional one. The Real offers not merely grace but hope. Such a religious viewpoint may not seem unusual to us because we are so familiar with it. But it is startling to those who are not in the two traditions. It is not easy to accept - beyond verbal endorsement - by those who are part of the traditions, perhaps because freedom is such a demanding experience, as the Israelites discovered in the desert.

The third image is of Yahweh the Husband and Lover. One can find him especially in Osee and in parts of Jeremiah and Ezekiel. Three of the oracles of Osee picture the extent of Yahweh's "fixation" on his beloved people:

---

[1]*The Jerusalem Bible.* New York: Doubleday & Co., 1966 Deuteronomy 26: 5-9. ©1966 by Darton, Longman & Todd, Ltd. and Doubleday & Co., Inc.

When Israel was a child I loved him,
and I called my son out of Egypt.
But the more I called to them, the further they went
    from me;
they have offered sacrifice to the Baals
and set their offerings smoking before the idols.
I myself taught Ephraim to walk,
I took them in my arm;
Yet they have not understood that I was the one look-
    ing after them.

....

Yet I am Yahweh, your God since the days in the land
    of Egypt;
you know no God but me,
there is no other saviour.
I pastured you in the wilderness;
in the land of drought
I pastured them, and they were satisfied;
once satisfied, their hearts grew proud,
and so they came to forget me.

....

Israel, how could I give you up?
How could I treat you like Admah,
or deal with you like Zeboiim?
My heart recoils from it,
my whole being trembles at the thought.
I will not give rein to my fierce anger,
I will not destroy Ephraim again,
for I am God, not man:
I am the Holy One in your midst
and have no wish to destroy.
They will follow behind Yahweh;
he will be roaring like a lion –
how he will roar! –
and his sons will come speeding from the west;
they will come speeding from Egypt like a bird,

speeding from the land of Assyria like a dove,
and I will settle them in their homes
– it is Yahweh who speaks.[2]

The extraordinarily powerful anthropomorphic poetry
of these passages is a scandal to many modern theologians. How dare God talk that way! Bishop Robinson in
particular, we might imagine, would dearly like to see
these passages forgotten. Forget them we may, but we
do so at the risk of overlooking a profound and crucial
insight of the Jewish religious experience, an insight
which has led one contemporary scripture scholar to
suggest that the fantastic anthropomorphism of the incarnation is not so surprising in a religious tradition
of which Osee is a part.[3]

The fertility gods had been sufficiently put to rout.
Yahweh was now able to appropriate sexual imagery for
himself. Yahweh is deeply involved with Israel as a
husband is with a wife, but Israel was not just any kind
of wife. She was a harlot, unfaithful to Yahweh, whoring
around with false gods; but Yahweh's passion for his
bride was such that he simply could not give her up.
He desired her with a passion that her infidelity could
not cool. He permitted her to exercise a power over
him that aroused his longings for her even when she became a coarse and vulgar prostitute. Yahweh was
"hooked" on his bride. He could not have enough of her,
and his ardor for his bride could never be cooled, never
even dampened by her infidelities.

Sexual imagery is universal in the human religious
experience. But Yahweh as the cuckolded husband who
will not give up his love is a fantastic and even blas-

---

[2]*Ibid.* Hosea 11:1-3, 13:4-6, 11:8-12.

[3]Ulrich Mauser, "Images of God and Incarnation".
Interpretation, July, 1970.

phemous symbol. Sexuality was of course a hierophany,
a manifestation of divine power at work in the repro-
ductive processes of plants, men, and animals; but the
idea that it was also the image of the commitment of
God in humankind; indeed, the entrapment of God by his
creatures was and is fantastic. Not only is the Really
Real a Thou who cares for us and pursues us, it is now
even a Thou of whom it can be said that he is sexually
aroused in our presence: an idea which was shocking
to the Jews, profoundly scandalous to their neighbors,
and difficult enough for the Jansenists and the Puritans
in modern Christianity to give much credence to. The
Roman Christians of the fourth century took over the
spring fertility symbol of the union between lighted
candle and water and put it into the Easter ceremonies
to symbolize that when Christ rose from the dead he
consummated his union with his bride, the Church. It
was certainly clear to the fourth century Romans that
they were using a symbol of sexual intercourse in their
Easter services, and it would be clear to anyone who
knows anything about the symbols of the nature religions. But while the image was kept, its meaning has
been carefully repressed through the ages. Generations of clergy have enacted the intercourse symbol,
and generations of laity have watched it without realiz-
ing that it conveyed the extraordinary notion that God
feels so passionately towards his people that human
sexual arousal is but a pale imitation of that passion.

The fourth Old Testament image which we must ponder is of Yahweh making promises. There was the
vague promise to Adam in the garden; and the promise
to Noah that there would be no more floods; and the
promise to Abraham that he would raise for him a
great people – a promise that was renewed to the
Patriarchs after Abraham; and the promise to Moses
that he would lead the children of Israel out of Egypt;
and the promise to the Israelites that he would bring

them through the desert to a land flowing with milk and honey; and later promises made, particularly through the Prophets, of a messianic age in which there would be peace and plenty, and all nations would come to Jerusalem to honor Yahweh and his people. In the messianic age all men would gather around the banquet table in fraternity and happiness to enjoy the benefits that Yahweh would bring to them through his beloved people.

Israel would be the tree under which all the nations of the world will find shade; Zion will be the mountain to which all nations of the world will come to pay honor; a banquet will be laid out in Jerusalem at which all the nations of the world will find satiety. All the kings and peoples of the world will come to pay homage to Israel's king.

The nature of the eschatological kingdom remains vague, although in the long history of Israel from the promise to Abraham to the reference to the Son of Man in the book of Daniel, the imagery becomes richer and more spectacular. Yahweh is not only a Lover, not only a Covenanter who will not repent of his commitment, but he is also an Eschatologist promising salvation and a future kingdom. In the nature religions there was a tradition of the golden age, the age of Saturn, for example, when the kindly Sky-God kept order among his fellow deities and peace and plenitude on earth. There was also the conviction that Saturn was not dead but only slept, and that in some future age the golden years would return. However, the Greek mythological view of things, based as it was on a cosmology which saw the heavens in constant circular motion, necessarily believed that even if the golden age should return, it too would pass away again as the great wheel of the heavens continued revolving.[4]

---

[4]Apparently, much mythological imagery was based on the phenomenon of the "precession" of the heav-

But Yahweh's messianic age is not a return to anything. It is not paradise all over again, but something
much more splendid. There is not the slightest hint that
it will eventually pass away as the Great Wheel turns.
Furthermore, the arrival of the kingdom has nothing to
do with the turning of the heavens. It, rather, results
from the will of Yahweh to whom even the heavens must
be subject. Finally, eschatological time will not be different from time as we now know it. It will not be completely trans-historical; Israel, an historical people,
will stand in the middle of the messianic world. Yahweh's promises may be vague, but they are not mystical. They deal with this earth and the peoples of this
earth.

---

ens; that is to say, the 26,000 year cycle of the polar
star based on the fact that the earth's axis completes
one cycle every 26,000 years, much as though it were
a massive spinning top. The slow revolution of the
heavens on its 26,000 year cycle is marked every
2,000 years or so by a new constellation preceding
the sun into the sky on the morning of the vernal
equinox. It is that constellation which gives the name
to the world age which will last for 2,000 years.
There is some dispute at the present time as to
whether we are still in the sign of the fish or whether
we have moved into the sign of Aquarius the Water
Carrier. An Aquarian myself, I sometimes suspect
that this is not my age at all, but more likely the age
of Cancer the Crab. For further details about the
cosmology of the precession, see *Hamlet's Mill* by
Giorgio di Santillana and Hertha vod Dechend (Boston:
Gambit Press, 1969) and *Stonehenge Decoded* by
Gerald S. Hawkins and John B. White (New York:
Doubleday, 1965). Incidentally, the men who discovered and recorded the phenomenon of the precession
and who built the fantastic observatory at Stonehenge
without the benefits of writing or mathematics were
anything but howling barbarians - a thought which
might be kept at the back of our minds when we are
tempted to engage in temporal ethnocentrism and
view our myth-making ancestors as superstitious
savages. It is precisely the tool of the myth that
enabled archaic man to record, analyse and explain
astronomical phenomena.

Thus, in the Jewish tradition, Ultimate Reality is seen not merely as good but as gracious, not merely as gracious but also as salvific. If the evil in the world results from man's infidelity to Yahweh, it should not in the final arrangement of things overcome Yahweh's goodness. Quite the contrary, evil will be eliminated and only good will remain.

This is an extraordinarily optimistic reading of the human condition - the most optimistic to be found in any other religious tradition. All other solutions to the problem of good and evil end up with at best a balance between the two; a precarious balance that shifts as the Great Wheel turns. But in the Jewish tradition Yahweh has cracked the Great Wheel and promised not only that good will dominate evil, but that it will eliminate it. Graciousness will triumph over suffering, dignity over malignity, and, in some fashion or other, life over death - though this theme is quite obscure in Old Testament eschatology. The Jewish religious cultural system does not deny the existence of evil, but it asserts that evil is less than ultimate and is also transient. In the end of things there will only be good.

What, then, do these four images of Yahweh the Covenanter, the Liberator, the Husband and Lover passionately seeking his bride despite her infidelities, and the Eschatologist promising a messianic kingdom say to the ultimate questions that a man must ask. The Jewish response is that the Really Real is good, unmitigatedly good. It is a Thou who cares about mankind, cares about them with fidelity, and passion, and a Thou who will eventually eliminate evil from the world. As I have said before, you may not like Yahweh, but if you don't like him and do not wish to believe in him, then make sure you reject him for the right reasons. Tell Yahweh that you don't believe that reality is ultimately gracious, passionately and irrevocably gracious; so gracious that it will eventually eliminate all traces of evil. Don't be angry with Yahweh because he is occasionally described as though he were an irate desert prince. Do not be angry with him because he smote the Moabites and the Idomites and those horrendous Philistines. Don't be angry with him because occasionally he seemed just a bit sulky. Be angry with him, rather, because you don't believe in graciousness.

Not that it will do you much good, because whether you believe in Yahweh or not doesn't much matter. He still believes in you.

Chapter Four

THE SON

I T IS probably clear from the previous chapter how much a Semite religion Christianity really is. Yahweh the Covenanter, the Liberator, the Lover, the Eschatologist is in no way denied by the Christian mythology. There are a number of additions that Christianity makes, but these additions are, in a way, logical developments of the religious framework laid down in the religion of Yahweh. The critical difference is that Christianity holds that God's sin is even worse than it appeared in the Old Testament. Not only does he become involved in human affairs, he actually now manifests himself in human form.

In this manifestation there are contained a number of dramatic and even revolutionary new insights into the ultimate nature of the Real. The manifestation of God in Jesus adds four principal themes to the Jewish interpretive scheme: 1. The messianic age is already here. It is not yet completely fulfilled, perhaps, but it has already begun. 2. The messianic age is begun through the suffering of the Messiah. Salvation comes, therefore, through suffering. 3. Yahweh has inserted himself in our midst as a friend, and through his friendship guarantees us triumph over death. 4. He has also sent us on a messianic mission: to spread the Good News of the messianic age and of friendship and resurrection.

There are, then, four critical symbols in the Christian fulfillment of the religion of Yahweh:

1. The eschatological Son of Man turned Suffering Servant.
2. The cross and resurrection.
3. The Eucharistic assembly and the community it represents.
4. The command of Jesus to go and preach the Good News.

Just as you may, if you wish, dislike Yahweh, so it is also within your privileges to reject Jesus of Nazareth. But if you do reject him, make sure you do so for the proper reason. Don't turn him down because of papal infallibility, or birth control, or angels, or the virgin birth, or any of those reasons. Dislike him if you will because you don't believe that the messianic age has begun, because you don't believe that resurrection triumphs over death, because you don't believe that friendship is possible in the human community, and because you don't believe in any Good News and do not wish to be constrained to spread it.

Paul Ricoeur, the French philosopher, says that the genius of Christianity is to be found in the combination of the symbol of the Suffering Servant with the symbol of the messianic Son of Man. With this combination Christianity asserts its conviction that the messianic age began with an act of suffering in which evil apparently triumphed over good only to find itself routed at the very last moment when it least expected good to reappear. No wonder the Christian can exclaim with St. Paul in an "I told you so" tone of voice, "Oh, death, where is your victory? Oh, death, where is your sting?"

Let us take a closer look at these two myths as they are to be found in the Old Testament.

I gazed into the visions of the night.
And I saw, coming on the clouds of heaven,

one like a son of man.
He came to the one of great age
and was led into his presence.
On him was conferred sovereignty,
glory and kingship,
and men of all peoples, nations and languages be-
    came his servants.
His sovereignty is an eternal sovereignty
which shall never pass away,
nor will his empire ever be destroyed.[1]

....

Like a sapling he grew up in front of us,
like a root in arid ground.
Without beauty, without majesty (we saw him),
no looks to attract our eyes;
a thing despised and rejected by men,
a man of sorrows and familiar with suffering,
a man to make people screen their faces;
he was despised and we took no account of him.

And yet ours were the sufferings he bore,
ours the sorrows he carried.
But we, we thought of him as someone punished,
struck by God, and brought low,
Yet he was pierced through for our faults,
crushed for our sins.
On him lies a punishment that brings us peace,
and through his wounds we are healed.

We had all gone astray like sheep,
each taking his own way,
and Yahweh burdened him
with the sins of all of us.

---

[1]*op. cit.* Daniel 7:13-14.

Harshly dealt with, he bore it humbly,
he never opened his mouth,
like a lamb that is led to the slaughter-house,
like a sheep that is dumb before its shearers
never opening its mouth.

By force and by law he was taken;
would anyone plead his cause?
Yes, he was torn away from the land of the living;
for our faults struck down in death.
They gave him a grave with the wicked,
a tomb with the rich,
though he had done no wrong
and there had been no perjury in his mouth.

Yahweh has been pleased to crush him with suffering.
If he offers his life in atonement,
he shall see his heirs, he shall have a long life
and through him what Yahweh wishes will be done.

His soul's anguish over
he shall see the light and be content.
By his sufferings shall my servant justify many,
taking their faults on himself.[2]

The Christian assertion is that the Son of Man riding on the clouds in power and majesty is also the Suffering Servant, despised and most abject of men, and that he accomplished his victory precisely by becoming a Suffering Servant. Good Friday, then, can be said to represent the Suffering Servant dimension of Christian mythology, and Easter (incluing Ascension Thursday) represents the triumph of the Son of Man. Note well the order. It is the act of the Suffering Servant which makes possible the triumph of the Son of Man. The messianic age is introduced by his suffering and resur-

---

[2]*op. cit.* Isaiah 53: 2-11.

rection and will be completed when he returns again as the Suffering Servant become Eschatological Judge.

The Christian mythology, then, is claiming not merely that Reality is passionately gracious, but that it is willing to suffer for us in order that it might bring us life, and by this suffering guarantees not merely the generic triumph of good over evil but also a highly specific triumph of life over death; indeed, of our life over our death.

As I have said before, reject Jesus of Nazareth if you wish, but make sure you reject him for the real reason. Do not dismiss his own claim to resurrection as absurd, because that was only a minor absurdity compared to the fantastic absurdity of his claim that he has come to bring life to all men and that all men will rise from the dead. "He who believes in me shall never die, and I will raise him up on the last day." If you are going to be angry at Jesus of Nazareth be angry at him for the right reason, not because he claimed to work some relatively minor wonders, but because he claims to have worked the absolutely untoppable wonder - to have conquered death for the whole race. As Carl Braaten says:

> Unless we, too, grasp Jesus' resurrection as the eschatological occurrence, as the beginning of something really new, we end by dealing with it as a miracle in analogy with other miracles. Then we either affirm or deny it, without realizing how little it means either way. The resurrection of Jesus is not an answer to the question whether a dead man can return to life, but an answer to the question whether the crucified Jesus is now living in union with God, not only for himself, but as our representative who has gone ahead to prepare the way for us.[3]

---

[3]*op. cit.* Braaten, p. 77.

Mark it well. Jesus does not claim to have eliminated death completely. Just as he had to die, his followers had to die. Death may be ultimately an illusion, but proximately, it is still a terrifying reality. Man is, in Carl Braaten's words, "cracked open," but because of Jesus he believes that the cracking open is not the end of it.

The most familiar solution to the problem of death is to place the soul of man out of its reach. This is what Ernst Bloch calls the "extraterritoriality" of the core of existence (the soul) in relation to death and nothingness. Religions specialize in painting pictures against death. The idea of the immortality of the soul, of its transmigration, or whatever, has been since Plato the classic expression of this attempt to satisfy death with only the outer shell of the soul. But death wants and gets more than the outer shell. It penetrates to the inner core of existence, cracks it open, and takes all there is to take. The solution of Christian hope to the problem of death is not to try to negotiate a settlement, hoping that the enemy will be decent enough to acknowledge the infinite value of some immortal part that is 'extraterritorial', beyond its jurisdiction. The only extraterritoriality that Christian hope knows is the life of the resurrected Christ who brings victory through and beyond death. We cannot pluck any hope from death; we cannot deny death's reach and reality; we cannot count on a deathless element inside of us. Instead, we affirm the deadlines and finality of death as the inescapable outcome of our lives. But that is not all we do. We anticipate a new beginning. We look at death as that which has already once met its match. We see the darkness of our own death illuminated by the light of Easter. 'By his great mercy we have been born anew to a living hope through the resurrection of Jesus Christ from the dead.'[4]

---

[4] *Ibid.*, Braaten, p. 80.

But there is more to be said, for Jesus not only proclaimed that it was Yahweh's will that life triumph over death, and that this will would be carried out by his son becoming a Suffering Servant. Jesus also announced that he was beginning a community. (He used the word of his own time when he called it a "kingdom.") This community would bear the Good News of the promise of life. He would be with this community in some way until he returned again to fulfill completely the eschatological reality that had already begun. Indeed, this community of the promise would eventually reach to the ends of the earth and embrace all men in unity; a unity which would come through belief in him. And he would be present in the midst of that community not so much as a king or a ruler, but as a friend. For the Christian, then, the Really Real, the Ground of Being, the Ultimate, is the Absolute announced at the Last Supper: "Behold, I do not call you servant, I call you friend." This is the ultimate in the Christian blasphemy, for the Christian believes that Reality has become his friend.

Before he suffered so that he might rise, Jesus instituted a meal, a thanksgiving banquet which that band of brothers who were his friends would share with him on the day when the promise was completely fulfilled. This meal, this friendship gathering, this love feast was to symbolize the intimate unity between the Real and his friends and among the friends themselves. It was to provide them with strength for the mission on which they were sent.

If we are the friends of Reality, we are also his co-workers. Jesus sent his friends on a mission to proclaim the Good News to the world: that the Son of Man had become Suffering Servant and then the Son of Man once again, and that those who believed in him would never die. In the Christian faith, Ultimate Reality has made the success of his eschatological mission dependent on the cooperation of his friends. The slowness, the hesitancy, the timidity, the infidelity, the weariness, the cynicism of his friends cannot indeed defeat the plans of God; but they can delay them, postpone them. Jesus will return, but only when we have prepared the way. The Christian, then, piles blasphemy upon blaspehmy. He claims not merely that God is his friend, but also a friend who needs his help. That man needs God's help is a truism, but that God needs man's help is a blasphemy that only Christians have attempted.

This, then, is the final step in the Christian interpretive scheme. We assert that the Really Real is in love with us, that he has become our friend; a friend who showed his love for us by suffering and even by dying in order that together with him we might eventually triumph over our own death. He is a friend, finally, who depends upon our help to complete the work which he has started.

Whether this Christian interpretive scheme is true or not is a question which each man must decide for himself. I wrote this book not to argue with you about its truth, but simply to present it to you so that you can make up your mind whether or not it is really too good to be true. The least I demand is that you face it for what it is, and do not try to escape its challenge by lapsing into arguments about whether Christ was really a God, or how can we know that the New Testament is telling us the truth? These may be the issues that were raised in your apologetics course in college, but they are relatively minor compared to the essence of the Christian message.

Was Jesus really God? To say that he was so totally and completely God that there was nothing human about him is false, both to the obvious intent of the scriptures and to the whole Christian theological tradition. (Indeed, a heresy called "adoptionism" was condemned for defending just such a position.) On the other hand, to assert that he was man like other men is also false, both to the obvious intent of the scriptures and to the profound experience of the early Christian community. He claimed to be *God's son* and in a way which no other man was God's son. He claimed to manifest God's plans and God's love in a way which no other man could manifest such plans and love. He claimed that those who saw him saw the father in heaven, that those who knew him knew the father in heaven.

Complex theological explanations have been developed to account for the extraordinary phenomenon of Jesus. It is appropriate that we be concerned with such explanations. It is absolutely essential that we assert both the humanity and the divinity of Jesus; but it is equally essential that we do not permit concern over the precise sorts of explanations behind that assertion to blind us to the message about the nature of the Real which the assertion symbolizes. Jesus is both God and man; not because it's fun to be both God and man; not because it's a nice test to put our faith to, to claim that he is both God and man; not because it provides an interesting problem for theologians to ponder over; but because the unity of divinity, and humanity in Jesus is a manifestation of the nature of the Real. It is a way of conveying to us what the world and life is all about and what our nature and destinies are. The manifestation of God in Jesus symbolizes both how far God's love for us has gone, and how much we may hope for because of that love. Carl Braaten summarizes the Christian conviction about how much man can hope for:

The hope of resurrection concerns the individual. In an age of collectivism the tendency is to translate individual hope into the social process. But the promise of a better society in the future is not a real fulfillment of the individual, as long as an individual is not reducible to his social function. A person is more than his social role. Resurrection hope, as the Bible proclaims it, is pressing on toward a totally human and fully personal fulfillment. On the other hand, hope is not limited to a fulfillment of individual persons. The world of nature makes it understandble that resurrection hope will rebel against every doctrinal restriction which sets fixed limits to its vision. Can a hope that is nourished by the promise of Christ's resurrection and filled with agapeic love ever err on the side of hoping too much?

Jesus' resurrection makes our history the time for hope. This hope is anchored in God's future, which has been revealed in raising Jesus from the dead. Since this future is not only the future of our present but the future of our past, because our present will also join our past as that which is no more. Christians remember the past hopefully as that which is reconciled to the present from the power of their common future. The power of God to raise the dead includes the power to gather up the broken, unfulfilled past into a new creation, so that at the end 'God may be everything to every one.'[5]

But one more question remains, albeit, a question which like so many others is more concerned with a non-issue than a real issue: can we believe the New Testament? Does it represent an accurate account of what Jesus did and said, or is it something that the early Christians made up?

The simplest answer to the question is that of course the early Christians made it up. It does not in any sense purport to be a videotape of what Jesus did and said. It is not a scientific and historically documented biography of Jesus. It is rather an account of what the very early Christians believed about Jesus. It records their

---

[5]*Ibid.* pp. 80-81.

interpretive scheme, their faith, their reading of the manifestation of God in Jesus. It represents their *experience* of Jesus and doesn't really purport to be anything else than that. It is unquestionably an accurate and valid account of how the Christians of the first century interpreted the experience of what they perceived to be the manifestation of God in Jesus. The New Testament is mythological in the sense we have been using the term in this book. It is an explanation and an interpretation of the Event of Jesus of Nazareth; it is not an impartial and unbiased scholarly account of the facts of his life.

A good deal of time and energy has been put in in the last several decades in "demythologizing" the New Testament. This is in its own way a valuable scientific contribution, insofar as it is an attempt to discover what precisely the objective historical element in the biblical story is. But demythologizing the scripture is merely an academic exercise if at the end the scholar feels that he has done all that is necessary, and that there is no need for him to pay any attention either as a scholar or as a person to the message that the books of the New Testament attempt to convey.

I am not suggesting that we do not know a good deal of the facts of Jesus' life. Early New Testament criticism was inclined to the conclusion that practically no authentic biographical information was to be found in the gospel stories; but in more recent years, passage after passage is restored to the category of "historical" information. However, we must realize that the importance of the basic message of the New Testament, the basic witness the early Christians made to the intervention of God in history in the person of Jesus, does not depend on the important but relatively secondary games that New Testament scholars play. Indeed, properly understood, the work of such scholars helps us to understand the message more clearly, and those

who view New Testament criticism as a game of de-
bunking show how out of contact they are with what
scripture scholars really do.

Do we have the message that Jesus delivered? The
answer would be that we surely do not have instant re-
play of that message, though we also certainly have accounts of his words and deeds that must be fairly close
to what actually happened. What we do have is the message that the early Christians received. The issue once
again is not whether the message of hope, the interpretive scheme which claims that the Ultimate Reality
wishes to be our intimate friend, is recorded in the
Scripture exactly the way Jesus delivered it. The basic
question is, rather, whether we are prepared to accept
or reject such an interpretive scheme as one according
to which we want to live. Whether we accept it or not,
as I have said repeatedly, is up to us; but if we reject
it let's reject it because it is blasphemous, or too good
to be true, or incredibly hopeful, and not because we
have doubts about whether St. John recorded the actual
words of Jesus or whether St. Mark might have arranged his account of events somewhat to fit the theme
he was presenting.

Carl Braaten has an excellent description of what the
New Testament is about:

> The whole New Testament speaks of the event for
> which the symbol of resurrection stands when it says
> that Jesus who was killed on the cross is no longer
> dead but is now alive. The event by which Jesus
> moved from the state of death to new life was called
> resurrection. There were, however, no witnesses of
> this event. What we can say for sure as a historical
> fact, in the currently narrowest sense of this term,
> is that there were witnesses who claimed to have
> seen Jesus after his death. The one who had been
> crucified appeared to them as the living Jesus. The

stories of Jesus' appearances and the witnesses' seeing do not all harmonize. Nevertheless, their common underlying datum is this occurrence of having seen none other than Jesus under new conditions of his presence and action. Those who had this experience reached the immediate conclusion that if the crucified Jesus is really living, God must have raised him from the dead. How could they have done so? They were in no more of a habit than we of calling someone dead alive. Yet this became something of which they could not be more convinced, so much so that they were ready to lay down their lives for it.[6]

The Christian believes, then, that the symbol called Jesus as it is conveyed to us in the books of the New Testament is a valid representation of the nature of reality. The Christian is committed to the notion that the meaning of the world and of life and of human destiny is to be found in the combination of the symbols of the Suffering Servant and the Son of Man, and in the fact that the reality represented by this combined symbol claims to be our friend who depends upon us for success in his mission of eliminating evil and death from the universe. If one believes in such an interpretation of reality, then one is Christian, and if one does not do so, then one is not a Christian, even though one may go to church or engage in appropriate religious behavior. In the time since Jesus we have shown a positive genius for escaping the issue, for trying to focus on secondary questions and trivial complications so that we need not face up to the blinding light of the Good News. If we once let that light shine upon us, then we have no choice but to accept it, because he

---

[6]*Ibid.* p. 76.

who commits himself to Jesus of Nazareth and the vision of Reality that he represents, commits himself both to cross and to resurrection, to suffering and hope, to the most revolutionary and most optimistic faith the world has ever know. It seems so much easier just to be ordinary and to hedge one's bets. We do not wish to live as though Jesus is indeed the Son of God, but we're afraid to live as though he were not.

Chapter Five

THE HOLY SPIRIT

THE SPIRIT, appropriately enough, is the most ethereal of the images of God available to the Christian. Yahweh the father is vigorously present in the images of the Old Testament, and we can meditate for all our lives on the images of Jesus in the New. But about the Spirit we know rather little. We must be born again of him. He is the one that is sent as the advocate and comforter. He will be with us until the return of Jesus. He is to hold together the community of Jesus' friends – that band of brothers who eats the Eucharistic banquet until Jesus eats it with them once again in the heavenly father's home. But there are four images to which we must pay special attention: the Spirit as wind, fire, light, and strength.

In his conversation with Nicodemus, Jesus, perhaps listening to the wind blowing on the Judean hillside, told that sincere but puzzled Jewish nobleman that like the wind, the Spirit blows whither he will; and on Pentecost the Spirit arrived with a mighty swirl of wind much like a tornado. The wind is spontaneous, variable, and unpredictable: sometimes fierce, sometimes gentle; sometimes warm, sometimes cool; sometimes noisy, sometimes soft. The Spirit of God, these images seem to suggest, is a Spirit of great variety and diversity. He works not in limited, circumscribed, predictable ways; rather, he is most at home with a wide variety of human talents, interests, skills, and personalities. He appeals to that in a man which is most imaginative, most creative, most spontaneous, and most representative of the best which is in himself. You will not put the Spirit of God into a bottle, you will not tie him down to a timetable, you will not limit his operation by a system of laws, or by a formal organizational structure; you will not be able to constrain him to work with only certain kinds of personalities and certain specific organizational structures; he is restless and impatient with such human limitations. He blows whither he will, touching the very depths of each personality with which he comes in contact. Those who are wise listen for him both as he speaks in their own souls and as he speaks to them through others whose hearts he has already moved.

He is a Spirit of enthusiasm, this windy Spirit of ours. Scripture scholars tell us that the principle scene of St. Luke's account of Pentecostal Sunday is that the Apostles' hitherto rather dour and constricted characters came alive with an ecstasy of enthusiasm. In fact, so turned on were they by the fierce wind of the Spirit, that many onlookers were convinced they had drunk too much wine. The Spirit had touched the very core of their being and unleashed the fierce, vigorous passions of their personalities.

The Christian believes that this is what the Spirit can do for him, too, though most of us manage to resist the Spirit's attempts to turn us on, and if comparison is forced upon us we would much rather behave as the Apostles did before Pentecost rather than after. It would not be at all appropriate for people to suggest that we had been carried away by our religious enthusiasm.

In the Christian conviction that the Spirit is wind we have, I think, the symbol of our faith that demands the very best in each of our personalities to which Ultimate Reality is appealing. God does not want us to destroy our talents, our visions, our energies, or our interests; even though for hundreds of years many Christians, particularly novice masters, mother superiors, and other such types, seemed to be persuaded that it was the essence of the Christian life to destroy that which was most spontaneous in man. But the great thinkers of the Catholic tradition such as Thomas Aquinas and Ignatius of Loyola realized that man must listen very carefully to the Spirit as he speaks, and he speaks to us, of course, usually not with a tornado, but through the promptings of that which is the best in our selfhood. It may have taken the insights of modern psychology to help us to understand what is meant by the image that the Spirit of God is a fierce wind which stirs us into enthusiasm, but now at least we know the wind of the Spirit works through the strength and resources, the vigor and the persistence of our own selfhood. It may be difficult at times to know what is really the best in ourselves, though St. Ignatius' rules for listening to the Spirit are as good as any that have been developed since, but it has never been especially easy to catch the Spirit's voice, not unless man has first disciplined himself to hear what the Spirit is really saying. Contemporary psychology has helped us to understand what the Scriptures ought to have made very clear. It is not selfishness nor ambition which prevents us from listening to the voice of the Spirit; it is rather fear, timidity, and lack of faith both in God and in ourselves. On the day of the first Pentecostal boogaloo it was precisely these failings of the Apostles that the Spirit of God overcame.

The second image of the Spirit is fire. He appeared on the scene at Pentecost in tongues of flame; flame which recalled Yahweh conversing with Moses in the burning bush, and yearning with passion for his people. The Spirit is the spirit of love, fierce, consuming love, which breaks through barriers of timidity, distrust, and suspicion; drives us on to heights of effort and courage and refuses to permit us to rest so long as there is work yet to be done. Christianity is a religion of passion; or at least it ought to be, and to the extent that Christians become passionless people, they are not true to their religion nor to the Spirit of God which keeps that religion alive and on fire until Jesus returns to lead us to the banquet table of his father. Whenever Christians become pale, vapid, lukewarm, dull and uninteresting, they have lost touch with the Spirit; they have turned their backs on the consuming passion which ought to mark them from other men. The Christian belief that God is a spirit of fire and flame symbolizes our conviction that we must respond to Reality with a passion something like that with which it pursues us. The Spirit has been sent to stir up passionate response within us. St. Paul tells us that the Spirit speaks to our spirit, meaning that the flame of God's love speaks to the hunger or faith and love that is in each of our personalities. We are, of course, able to resist that hunger, to turn back the Spirit, to even throw cold water on his fire, for the Spirit does not take away our freedom. We can even deny that his fire exists, for that is an easy way to excuse ourselves from passionate commitment to life and reality. But let us not kid ourselves. He who denies the Spirit of God is fire denies an essential component of the Christian myth.

The Spirit of God is also light. Jesus said that he came to bring light to the world, and that we who are his followers should not hide our lamps under a bushel. The community of friends he established to spread his Good News was commissioned to be a light shining on the mountaintop. The Spirit of God energizes the light of the Church, but the light of the Church is love. Jesus said, "By this shall all men know that you are my disciples: that you have love for one another." It is the quality of human relationships inside the Church that makes it a light to the nations – a searching beacon illuminating the darkness of the valleys around them. And it is God's Spirit encouraging and reinforcing love among members of the Church that provides the power and the energy to keep the light on.

The Christian notion that God's Spirit is a spirit of light represents our conviction that the Really Real is most fully present among us when we love another, when we put aside the barriers of suspicion, distrust, narrowness, and hatred to open ourselves out to one another in affection, trust, openness, and friendship. Honesty compels us to note that there is substantially less friendship in the Church than one would hope for; that, indeed, Jesus' prediction that all men would know that we were his disciples by the quality of our love for one another is a prediction which has apparently yet a long way to go before it is fulfilled. Again, the Spirit of God respects our freedom. If we do not want to love, if we want to hide behind our distrust and suspicion and fear, then we are perfectly free to do so, but let us not justify such hiding by calling it Christianity; it is, rather, a perversion of the Christian message. Ultimate Reality is most present among men, the depths of the universe are most clear and understandable when men are brave enough to take the chance of loving one another.

Finally, God's Spirit is the spirit of strength. In his farewell discourse to His Apostles, Jesus repeatedly promised what the old translation called, quite poetically, the Paraclete, and what newer translations, somewhat less vividly, call the Comforter or the Advocate.[1] The point of the coming of the Paraclete was that he was being sent to sustain the Apostles through the dangers, the weariness, the trials, and the difficulties of spreading the Good News. Jesus was going to the heavenly father, but he was not leaving his followers

[1] Of course nobody really knew quite what a Paraclete was, but it still was a marvelous sounding word.

alone or unaided in the struggles that they were to face. He did not want to take him out of the world, but he wished to protect them from the world's evil, and the Spirit would come to inspire them as to what to say when they were hauled before kings and governors, refresh them when they were tired and weary, strengthen them when they were discouraged, cheer them up when they were depressed, and urge them on when they were tempted to give up.

When a Christian states his faith in the Holy Spirit, the Paraclete, he makes what is in one way the most difficult act of faith of all, for he asserts that discouragement if persisted in is not justified, and that as T. S. Eliot put it, "Disillusion if persisted in is the ultimate illusion." Discouragement, disillusion, weariness, are luxuries which the Christian by his faith has decided he cannot permit himself. The Really Real has not only asserted his love, but has also rather disturbingly assured us that we will have the strength and vigor we need to respond to that love, to surrender to it, and then to bear witness to it to the ends of the earth.

A most inconsiderate and thoroughly pushy thing it is for the Ground of Being to do, but the Christian is still stuck with this conviction as much as he would like to be rid of it: God cares for him so much that he even provides him with the strength to respond. To put the matter more abstractly, Reality is so benign that it provides us with the resources we need to live benign lives; that is to say, lives of gracious response.

Chapter Six

CONCLUSIONS

IN THIS BOOK I have spoken of God. I have asserted that God is man's mythological way of stating his faith about the nature of Reality; of explicating the answers he once gave himself about the meaning and purpose of life, the triumph of life over death and of good over evil, and of how the good man ought to live.

I have pointed out that the Christian interpretive scheme as represented by the pushy, Jewish God of the Christians is a radical and revolutionary meaning system, one that is incredibly hopeful and blasphemously familiar in its attitude toward Reality. I believe that Christianity can be organized around several images of God:

Yahweh the Covenanter
Yahweh the Liberator
Yahweh the Jealous Husband
Yahweh who promises the messianic banquet
The Son of Man turned Suffering Servant
The Crucified and Risen Jesus
The Host at the first Eucharistic banquet
The Leader who sends His friends forth to bring the
    Good News to the world
The Mighty Wind of the Spirit
The Tongues of Fire
The Blazing Light on the mountaintop
The Strength-Bearing Paraclete

In all the images of God we have described in this book one important theme is never absent: <u>God is involved</u>. Yahweh in the desert, Jesus the Suffering Servant, the dazzling, dancing Spirit all are intimately involved in human history and in human growth. The best of contemporary Catholic theologians quite rightly insist that our God is not an "Outsider", sitting aloof on his throne passing judgement on, or even playing games with his creatures. God is rather an "Insider." Indeed, everything we know about him we know from his dealings with us. The immense contributions of theologians like Karl Rahner and Gregory Baum is their insistence that God is deeply involved in the growth of the human person. In Father Baum's words: "While we must speak of God as the destiny of man, summoning him forth towards friendship and truth we must also think of God as incarnate in Christ acting in history and as Holy Spirit alive in Christ and in all men joined to him in Faith".[1]

God is, as Baum remarks, what happens to man on the way to becoming human. And Edward Schillebeeckx says that God is the Good News that humanity is possible. I would go further and say that Christ is the even Better News that friendship is possible. According to Baum, "'God exists' means that man is always more than man. It means that wherever people are, something new happens. *It means that man is alive by a principle that transcends him, over which he has no power, which summons him to surpass himself and frees him to be creative.*"[2]

The "psychological" or "existential" approach of this kind of theology results from a reconsideration and a reformulation of traditional doctrine in light of

---

[1]Gregory Baum, *Man Becoming: God in Secular Experience* (New York: Herder and Herder, 1970), p. 179.

[2]*Ibid.* p. 185.

contemporary personalist philosophy and social science. God is seen as a gift, a surprise, a promise of a
future with possibility, a triumph of life over death not
merely in the final resurrection, but also in the thou-
sand resurrections of man's triumph over the many
deaths, big and small, which he must face in the process of human growth. Man comes close to God precisely to the extent that he becomes more himself; and he
becomes more himself to the extent that he responds
to God's generosity with generosity of his own.

This new theological emphasis is filled with great
possibilities. Indeed I think that Baum's book *Man
Becoming* is one of the most important books of our
time. We must remember as we read the works of such
theologians that they are not distorting Christianity to
fit the fashions of contemporary existentialism. On the
contrary, the existentialist perspective helps us to see
more deeply what was always present in the Christian
meaning system. The symbols from that meaning system that we have described in this book seem to cry
for existentialist interpretation. If our God is a God of
love, it inevitably follows that we become more like
him when we increase our capacity to love. If he has
involved himself in a love affair with us, he is obviously summoning us to a love affair with our fellow men.
The existentialist theologians simply have at their dis-
posal a good deal more sophisticated understanding of
the dynamics of love. It would be foolish to dismiss
this understanding as unimportant and equally foolish
to think that ours was the first era to understand that
Christianity is essentially a call to grow in love and a
promise of a gracious future.

I shall not attempt now, as I have not attempted in
the rest of the book, to persuade you that this is what
Reality is actually like; that the Christian symbols are
an accurate representation of the nature of the universe. I will merely insist, as I have all along, that if

you turn your back on Christianity you do so because you find such notions incredible, or blasphemous, or far too optimistic, or disgracefully hopeful. Reject Christianity if you will out of motives of cynicism; turn away from it because you believe that Reality is malign and punitive; choose a God that is vindictive, or cantankerous, or forgetful, or determined to keep man in his place, if such a God is more to your choosing. If you can't accept the idea that love is at the core of the universe, then that, as I have said before, is your privilege. If you do not believe that the Absolute passionately wants to be our friend and our lover, then by all means reject such a seemingly absurd notion. If you do not believe that we have the enthusiasm, and the strength, and the courage, and the creativity to love one another as friends, then quickly cast such an incredible idea into the trash can. And if you think it is ridiculous to believe that life will triumph over death, then don't bother with Christianity, because you can't be a Christian unless you believe that.

Thus, there are many good reasons for rejecting Christianity, excellent, splendid reasons; but, for the love of heaven, don't try to persuade me that you reject it because you can't believe in God, or in the divinity of Jesus, or in the resurrection, or papal infallibility, or the virgin birth, or angels, or God knows what other doctrinal formulation of the Christian message. And certainly don't complain to me about the Catholic schools, or what a nun did to you in sixth grade, or of how your mother made you go to confession every Saturday, or what a priest said to you when you and your fiance came to make arrangements for marriage. I do not wish to defend as absolute and beyond further development all dogmatic formulations, nor do I want to defend the bizarre aberrations in which Christians have engaged in in the past, engage in in the present, and will certainly engage in in the future. But I wish to insist that neither doctrinal formulations, however important they may be, nor the behavior of Christians, no matter how scandalous it may be, has anything to do with the ultimate themes of the Christian message. These themes deserve to be faced and judged for what they are - a comprehensive, systematic explanation of what the human condition is all about - a wild, bizarrè, incredibly hopeful explanation, an explanation, which begins with thunder and lightning on Sinai, continues with the mighty tornado of Pentecost, and will persist down through the ages until the Son of Man, who is also Suffering Servant, comes back to serve the dessert of the messianic banquet.

But at least if you do not wish to like this God of mine, acknowledge that from my point of view I cannot be expected to waste much time having sympathy for you. I refuse to sympathize with you not because I feel that you are destined for perdition; on the contrary, I suspect just the opposite. You can keep on running, but the Hound of Heaven will catch up with you; you can keep on hiding, even in the belly of the whale, but from his throne on Sinai, Yahweh can see not only the depths of the ocean, but the depths of the human heart; and you can keep on refusing to dance with our wheeling and dealing Spirit, but the music will rise to a crescendo, the dance goes on, and the Old Ghost will get you yet.